DATE DUE

DEC 1 6 1982		
MAR 3 0 1983		
DEC 1 0 1983		
NOV 1 6 1989		
APR 1 5 1990		
MAY 2 4 1990		
NOV 2 2 1993		
MAY 1 4 1994		
NOV 3 1994		

DEMCO NO. 38-298

THE MEDIA AND POLITICAL VIOLENCE

THE MEDIA AND POLITICAL VIOLENCE

Richard Clutterbuck

Foreword by
Sir Robin Day

First published 1981 by
THE MACMILLAN PRESS LTD
London and Basingstoke
Companies and representatives
throughout the world

ISBN 0 333 31484 0

Typeset in Great Britain by
Scarborough Typesetting Services
and printed in Hong Kong

To Louise

Contents

PART II   DEMONSTRATIONS AND THE
INSTITUTIONS OF LAW AND ORDER

PART III   TERRORISM

PART IV WHAT IS TO BE DONE?

Foreword
by Sir Robin Day

Unlike so many of the academics who write about violence and the media, Richard Clutterbuck is by training a soldier, not a sociologist. At the age of fifty-five he brought to a second profession (in academic research and teaching) the experience of a distinguished military career. He always gets annoyed with me when I call him 'General' on the box. He much prefers to be known as Dr Clutterbuck, MA (Cantab.), PhD (London), Lecturer in Politics at Exeter University since 1972, rather than as a retired soldier (Major-General Clutterbuck, CB, OBE, Colonel-Commandant of the Royal Engineers from 1972 to 1977).

But it is Dr Clutterbuck's military background which gives to his book a directness and clarity in refreshing contrast to the trendy, pretentious jargon which is too often seen in books which publishers pour forth about the media.

This is an important and controversial book. It is important because it grapples with the most difficult question which those who work in the media (especially television) have ever had to face: 'How, in a liberal democracy, can we ensure that television and the press do not become allies of terrorism and of other forms of political violence?' For its examination of that fundamental but neglected question Dr Clutterbuck's book deserves to be read and studied, not only by everyone with responsibility in the media and in politics, but by everyone (and this must mean most of us) who is concerned about the increasing threat to the peace and stability of our democracy from political violence of one degree or another.

It is a controversial book because some of its conclusions and recommendations will be hotly opposed, even by many of those who may be in sympathy with Dr Clutterbuck's analysis. I for one do not agree with some of his conclusions. For example, I shall enjoy some heated but friendly arguments with Dr Clutterbuck about his proposal for an Institute for the Mass Media (IMM)

which, like the GMC or the Law Society, would have disciplinary
powers, if necessary by legislation, over newspapermen and broadcasters, whose registration with the IMM would be compulsory.
Breach of the IMM code would mean that the guilty editor or
broadcaster would be 'struck off the register' like a crooked
solicitor or a doctor who seduces a patient. That does not appeal to
me at all.

I shall also enjoy taking Dr Clutterbuck to task for his proposal
that legislation should be introduced to give chief constables the
discretion *without the Home Secretary's authority* to declare a
'local state of emergency' for up to six hours. Is this a power which
chief constables want?

However strongly you may disagree with his conclusions and
recommendations you are likely to be absorbed by his detailed
accounts (enlivened by personal interviews with leading participants, such as Arthur Scargill) of events which were climacterics of
the turbulent and violent 1970s: Saltley, Grunwick, the 'Winter of
Discontent' in 1978/9. And, in a very different category, the
appalling terrorist outrages of Irish or Middle East origin.

Dr Clutterbuck's analysis of such events raises some very interesting questions: is he right in suggesting that the BBC television interview with one of Airey Neave's INLA assassins may well
have goaded the IRA to assassinate Lord Mountbatten? Is he right
to suggest that ITN's action in smuggling a camera to cover the
back of the Iranian Embassy was wrong, and could have endangered the SAS operation? Was the Chief Constable of Birmingham right to have closed the gates of the Saltley Coke Depot in
1972? Was this a deplorable surrender to the brute force of Scargill's massed pickets, or was it the only wise and sensible thing to do
in the circumstances? Did the British press behave with 'appalling
irresponsibility' in the early stages of the kidnapping of Annabel
Schild and her mother in Sardinia?

But because Dr Clutterbuck's book is so controversial in its conclusions, and so important in its analysis of the problem, I hope it
will be widely and seriously discussed. I hope it will be made the
starting point for media seminars and conferences, which too
often ramble around the subject without any clear basis for argument. I particularly urge that Dr Clutterbuck's book should be the
subject of critical discussion at meetings of the kind arranged by
BAFTA (the British Academy of Film and Television Arts), at
meetings of the NUJ and the IOJ, and at seminars arranged by the

BBC and the IBA. The book should be debated (and defended by Dr Clutterbuck in person) at gatherings such as the Edinburgh Festival, which in recent years has included a programme of media discussions attended by leading practitioners and media executives.

Above all, this is a book whose subject should be debated in Parliament. If the Commons or one of its new Select Committees cannot find time, the House of Lords would be an admirable forum with expert contributions from peers with professional experience in the media, in the press, in the broadcasting authorities, and from others with ministerial experience of terrorism and political violence in all its different forms.

Dr Clutterbuck does me the honour of frequently quoting from my own writings. He adopts as a central theme of his argument the need to protect and defend what I have termed the 'Reasonable Society'. This is a concept which I have tried somewhat ineffectually to propagate. It lies at the root of my professional philosophy.

Dr Clutterbuck is not the kind of man who would expect me to repay his approval with undiluted praise for his book. A book is only worth criticising if it is worth reading. This book is certainly worth reading. More than that, it is a book to cause everyone concerned about the future of our democracy to think, and to think seriously.

Dr Clutterbuck's army days are over. But the soldier who turned in his uniform for an academic gown cannot resist a military metaphor to sum up the message of his book in its very last paragraph:

In the battle for survival of the reasonable society, the television camera is the super tank — the Queen of the Battlefield.

Let us make sure, as Dr Clutterbuck argues, that the heavy armour of television is on the side of reason and the democratic process.

ROBIN DAY

Preface

When working on my previous books, especially *Britain in Agony* and *Kidnap and Ransom*, I became more and more conscious of the influence of the media in situations of political violence. The first of these two dealt mainly with violent demonstrations and picketing and the politics behind them while the second dealt with terrorism. The television camera emerged as the most powerful weapon available in these modern forms of conflict — a weapon lying in the street available for either side to pick up and use.

Although there are many books about the effect of television on violence, they are mainly about social and criminal violence; there are also dozens of books about the media, professional, technical, psychological, sociological and political; I have mentioned some of these in the Introduction, but none focused to any extent on political violence.

I therefore set about trying to find out how far the media influenced the violent incidents I had studied (e.g. Saltley, Grunwick, Red Lion Square and Lewisham) or which arose while I worked (e.g. the 'Winter of Discontent', Southall and the Iranian Embassy siege). To what extent was publicity a primary aim of those instigating the incidents? Did they get their publicity and did it pay or rebound? Did the media only go because they expected violence? Did they then exaggerate it? Did the presence of the cameras encourage people to 'act up'? Did they increase violence or restrain it? Did the reporting of violence exacerbate the underlying conflicts, and did it make violence in future confrontations more or less likely? Did the media act so recklessly as to put lives at risk? If so, should they restrain themselves or be restrained and, if so, how? And what should we, the people, learn about how to live with the media?

The impetus to write a book often comes from a burning passion to make fundamental changes in society. Although I have commended some radical changes, mainly in the fields of industrial democracy, electoral reforms and other ways of restoring power to the people through Parliament (see *Britain in Agony*), I am more concerned still to retain what is good, notably the framework of parliamentary democracy and the rule of law. This may not be fashionable among writers but it is still, I think, fashionable amongst the majority of readers, who look around the world and find other systems worse. Unashamedly I want to sustain, to use Sir Robin Day's term, the 'Reasonable Society'.

I have been lucky in that my daily work has constantly over-lapped my research for this book. My university students, whose persuasions range from the Monday Club to the Socialist Workers' Party, have been a constant stimulant, and an insurance against a generation gap. Outside the university I have been giving about 80 lectures each year to some 500 police officers, mainly at inspector level, fresh from the streets, and to about 1000 army officers, virtually all of whom have served in Northern Ireland; also to another 1000 or so from industry, who have to grapple both with picketing and (especially those with overseas interests) with the threat of terrorism. I never give a lecture without at least a 40-minute discussion period and I have learned more from my discussions with these 2500 practical professionals every year than I could have learned from a whole shelf of books in the library.

I have also, for the past six years, been a member of the BBC's General Advisory Council, which brings me into contact four times a year with the BBC's management, not to mention my fellow Council members, often to discuss the kind of problems covered in this book. I am also a fairly frequent participant in television and radio programmes about politics and violence, which I have there-fore discussed with a lot of practising producers and journalists.

Concurrently, I also had the good fortune to supervise Alan Hooper during his work on an MA thesis at Exeter University. He was welcomed as a fly on the wall by both the BBC and ITN during the production of news, current affairs and documentary pro-grammes, interviewed many leading editors (including those of BBC News, ITN, the *Daily Telegraph* and the *Sun*) and producers and journalists. His work is due to be published shortly after this book under the title of *The Military and the Media*. The mere formal acknowledgements in my notes do not begin to do justice to what I learned from this, and anyone interested in the media should read his book.

It must be clear from the above that there are far more people who have helped me than I can possibly acknowledge. I must, however, express particular gratitude to some of the busiest ones who have given so generously of their time: Lord Scarman and Sir Robert Mark, whose wisdom I used as my starting base; Chief Constables Sir Kenneth Newman, John Alderson and Peter Imbert (who developed the art of hostage negotiating at Spaghetti House and Balcombe Street); Bill McGookin and Dave Hanna of the RUC Press Office in Belfast; of the BBC, Sir Michael Swann, the late Sir Charles Curran, Sir Ian Trethowan, Richard Francis and Alan Protheroe (who handled 'television's finest hour' at the Iranian Embassy siege), all of whom gave up a lot time to me. Of the large number of working journalists who have helped me I must single out Sir Robin Day, who taught me a great deal on the job and also found time for philosophical discussions on my subject. Kate Adie, of BBC Television News, Julian Norwich of London Weekend Television and Joe Rogaly of the *Financial Times* (who wrote the superb instant Penguin on *Grunwick*) also contributed generously and frankly.

I owe an unrepayable debt to my successive research assistants, Louise Perry and Gail Joughin. Louise, ex-policewoman and law graduate, bore the brunt of the research period; she threw herself unreservedly into the project and was a constant source of inspiration and encouragement. This book is dedicated to her. Gail, who followed Louise for the write-up phase, is a strong character with a huge sense of humour; she has been a penetrating researcher and a forthright and constructive critic tearing into my logic and ripping apart my prose, to the enormous improvement of both. That I should have been blessed with the stimulus of friends like Louise and Gail is one of my luckiest breaks of all.

Finally, I want to thank Sir Robin Day for the compliment that he has paid to my book by writing the foreword to it. When I sent him the typescript and asked him if he would consider doing this, I said that I expected him to disagree with some of my proposals and knew that he would say so. He has — with a characteristic zest that is just what the book needs, because the problem it tackles is one to which the best answers will only be found by controversy and discussion. Sir Robin began this discussion in his own broadcasts and writings and I have taken it from there. If this book provokes further argument as lively as that in his foreword it will have achieved its object.

Exeter   RICHARD CLUTTERBUCK
December 1980

List of Abbreviations

ACAS	Advisory, Conciliation and Arbitration Service
ANL	Anti-Nazi League
AP	Associated Press
APEX	Association of Professional, Executive and Computer Staff
ASLEF	Amalgamated Society of Locomotive Engineers and Firemen
ASU	Active Service Unit
ATV	Associated Television Corporation
AUEW	Amalgamated Union of Engineering Workers
BBC	British Broadcasting Corporation
BMA	British Medical Association
CBI	Confederation of British Industry
CID	Criminal Investigation Department
CO	Commanding Officer
CPGB	Communist Party of Great Britain
ENG	Electronic news gathering
EPA	Employment Protection Act
GAC	General Advisory Council (BBC)
GMC	General Medical Council
GMWU	General and Municipal Workers' Union
HMSO	Her Majesty's Stationery Office
IBA	Independent Broadcasting Authority
ICI	Imperial Chemical Industries
IMG	International Marxist Group
IMM	Institute for the Mass Media (proposed)
INLA	Irish National Liberation Army

IOJ	Institute of Journalists
IPC	International Publishing Corporation
IRA	Irish Republican Army
IRSP	Irish Republican Socialist Party
IS	International Socialists
ITN	Independent Television News
ITV	Independent Television
MP	Member of Parliament
NAFF	National Association for Freedom
NCB	National Coal Board
NCCL	National Council for Civil Liberties
NF	National Front
NICRA	Northern Ireland Civil Rights Association
NUJ	National Union of Journalists
NUM	National Union of Mineworkers
NUR	National Union of Railwaymen
NUT	National Union of Teachers
OB	Outside broadcast
PC	Police Constable
PR	Public relations
PA	Press Association
QC	Queen's Counsel
RTE	Radio Telefis Eireann
RUC	Royal Ulster Constabulary
RUSI	Royal United Services Institute
SAS	Special Air Services
SPG	Special Patrol Group
SWP	Socialist Workers' Party
TGWU	Transport and General Workers' Union
TUC	Trades Union Congress
TV	Television
UPI	United Press International

UPW	Union of Postal Workers (now Union of Communication Workers)
UVF	Ulster Volunteer Force
UWC	Ulster Workers' Council
UXB	Unexploded bomb

Introduction

Great Britain (as distinct from Northern Ireland) is high if not top in at least three league tables: for the past century we have enjoyed what must be one of the lowest rates of political violence in the world, measured in terms of deaths due to riots and terrorism; we have the highest degree of public co-operation with the police, enabling them to maintain public order without carrying arms; and we have what is generally recognized as the best broadcasting organization in the world coupled with a press which can certainly compete with any other in terms of its freedom and quality.[1]

There is a connection between the ethics and quality of our media and our record of non-violence. Nevertheless, like any team at the top of its league, we can only hope to stay there if we constantly criticize, refine and improve. The main generators of civil unrest in any country are corruption, abuse of police or other official power, brutality behind the scenes in police and prison cells and unfair harassment and detention. The best guard against these, though nothing can wholly eliminate them, is the searchlight of investigative journalism by a free press. These abuses have grown in almost every society which has not had a free press to keep them in check, and such societies have in the end usually tried to purge themselves with a more or less violent revolution or *coup d'état* but to no avail as the revolutionary regime is usually even more oppressive than the one it replaced. Of all the countries which are without a free press, from Marxist to military dictatorship, none has been in existence in its present form for even one man's lifespan; the longest survivor is the Soviet Union which had its 63rd birthday in 1980.

This brings us to a fourth league of which Britain is unarguably top. While our political, social and economic system has evolved through the strains of the first industrial revolution, the Napoleonic wars and two world wars, we have not had a single violent or unconstitutional change in our system of government (by the Monarch in an elected Parliament) for some 300 years – i.e. since 1688

1

(or some would claim 1660). Our nearest rival in this league, the USA, is about 100 years behind us. We probably underrate this blessing. The history of France, Russia, China and of many Latin American countries suggests that the sum of human misery during and after revolutionary change has been greater than anything we have had to endure other than in two externally inflicted world wars, and in some cases even greater than that. An unsuccessful attempt at revolution or a long period of internal conflict and chaos can be just as bad, when the people's fear for the security of their families and of their means of livelihood leads them to rally to a strong man who will bring them order at the expense of civil liberties. Carried into power by a reaction against chaos, Mussolini, Hitler and many Latin American dictators have enjoyed strong support from the majority of their people, but at a heavy price, and none of them have lasted for very long.

The safeguards of a democratic society which endures without suffering the cataclysmic horrors of revolution or a collapse of order are the same as those which give the individual a reasonable life within that society. Foremost amongst these are a strict legal limit on the number of years a government may govern without renewal of its mandate from the people and the maintenance of the rule of law by an independent judiciary, including laws which guarantee that if an individual has a grievance against any of the organs of the state, he or his family or friends will have a means of bringing it to public notice and of seeking redress in the courts. There are relatively few countries in the world where these apply.

Backed by such safeguards, parliamentary democracy has proved to be the best means yet devised to ensure that government remains answerable to public opinion and to maintain a pluralist society which can balance and accommodate the clash of opposing bodies of opinion within it. It is by its nature imperfect. In Britain, its main shortcomings have developed from the erosion of the power of Parliament by functional groups which become too powerful for a fair balance, including the financial institutions, the employers' associations, the trade unions and, more recently, the media themselves.

The way to overcome these shortcomings is not to supplant parliamentary democracy by a totalitarian system which would stifle the power of all the functional groups, above all the counter-acting power of a free and investigative press. The answer lies in restoring power to the people through Parliament, by making it more truly representative and more responsive to public opinion. There are many ways in which this can be done — by, for example, a better electoral system and the use of referenda and official public opinion polls by Parliament to seek proof of public support before it introduces controversial legislation.[2] The media themselves should play a major part in strengthening and reinforcing the institutions which make government responsive to the people and which maintain their civil liberties.

Sir Robin Day has thrown his weight unequivocally in favour of sustaining what he defines as a 'Reasonable Society'

What I am arguing will be regarded with contempt and derision by certain people, including some in the media and in the universities. There are those who devote their minds and their activities to propagating a very different set of ideas: that the Rule of Law is bourgeois establishment oppression, that parliamentary government is ritualized hypocrisy, that peaceful cooperation with the democratic system is surrender to the prevailing power-structure, that criminal violence of the most bestial kind can be morally justifiable. If you start being intellectually seduced by that kind of argument, then you are on the road to nothing but the jungle. In the absence of a world rule of law, the nation states of the world are still marching on that road. But within nation states, or at least within *our* nation state, which is what matters to me, we have chosen the path of reason, to establish that civilized order which is liberty under law and government by consent.[3]

This is patently the path preferred by the great majority of the British people, but the strength and durability of our institutions lies in the fact that 'those who devote their minds and their activities to propagating a very different set of ideas' are as free to propagate those ideas in the media as those who wish to sustain parliamentary democracy.[4]

Sir Ian Trethowan, Director-General of the BBC, has written, referring to both broadcasters and newspapermen: 'We all know that our own professional freedom and independence rest on Parliamentary democracy and the rule of law. But we also know . . . that a freedom must be exercised, albeit with care and responsibility, if it is not to invite erosion.'[5]

One of the tools which is used to destabilize parliamentary democracy and to poison the reasonable society is the political use of violence and disruption. Sir Robert Mark, shortly after his retirement as Commissioner of the Metropolitan Police in 1977 condemned it without reservation:

> I do not think that what we call 'crimes of violence' are anything like as severe a threat to the maintenance of tranquillity in the country as the tendency to use violence to achieve political or industrial ends. As far as I am concerned that is the worst crime in the book. I think it is worse than murder.[6]

Sir Robin Day also stressed the threat such violence posed to the survival of civilized order:

> Of late, that civilized order has been increasingly threatened by unreason and lawlessness, violence and terrorism. Television may well have been, if not the cause, a contributing influence. By reflecting, television may have inflamed. By depicting, television may have magnified. By projecting, television may have incited. By accentuating, television may have encouraged.[7]

Examples of all of these will be found in the case-studies in this book. In some cases the primary purpose of the violence was to attract publicity. In other cases the coverage of the violence had a shock effect which deterred or restrained subsequent violence, but more often, as Sir Robin Day suggests, the presence of the camera, or the hope of attracting its presence, tended to encourage or increase it.

Three kinds of violence — and the influence of the media upon them — will be examined in these case-studies: violence in industrial disputes; violence in political demonstrations; and terrorism. They will be considered only when the occasion for the violence has been to further a political aim.

The damage done by political violence lies in the poison which it injects into a democratic society (which may be its precise aim) rather than in the number of people killed or injured. Criminal violence — that is, violence in the course of a crime whose aim is purely personal gain — kills and injures far more people every year. That is not the subject of this book; nor is social violence except where such violence or its causes are exploited for political ends.

Thus the frustration of unemployment or the tension arising from racial conflict, especially amongst young people in inner-city areas, manifests itself in social violence (such as football hooliganism or the group violence of skinheads or Hell's Angels) but also provides the impetus for violent demonstrations on the streets. The raw material is the same. Football hooligans or skinheads are, typically, young people whose lives offer no other kind of satisfaction or outlet; many come from deprived backgrounds, did badly at school and have no job nor any hope of a job. Their only solace lies in their friends who are in the same boat. They have an inarticulated longing to be part of some group which has some 'clout', and in which they can have some pride. The only focus for group solidarity and pride may be the support of their city's football team. For their team to be beaten strikes at the root of their pride. To be taunted by the supporters of their hated and victorious rivals is beyond endurance — indeed to endure it without a fight is seen as a shameful surrender of virility.

This same kind of aggressive pride can, however, be harnessed for political purposes and this is done by the National Front (NF) which appeals to old-fashioned jingoism and replaces hatred for rival football supporters with hatred for racial minorities.

Racial conflict, though not in itself political, can be exploited no less effectively on the other side by such movements as the Socialist Workers' Party (SWP — see Chapter 5). Violent demonstrations will attract publicity and a primary aim may be to discredit the police, who are as fundamental as a free press in preserving parliamentary democracy and the rule of law.

Quite separately from this, the media themselves may sometimes be used, especially through documentaries and dramas about the police, the prison service and the law, to discredit these institutions with the same aim. A fundamental dilemma here lies in distinguishing between the duty to disclose and the desire to discredit. False or exaggerated accusations or dishonest 'documentary dramas' can be used with the intent not just to compel the police to deal with their rotten apples, but specifically to discredit them for political purposes. This dilemma, the distinction between honest disclosure and the desire to discredit, is discussed in Chapters 6, 7 and 8.

When embarking on the research for this book, the author asked Lord Scarman what he thought would be the likeliest causes of political violence in Britain in the years ahead. His answers were

racial conflict and industrial problems, especially unemployment.[8] Both can be exploited for political purposes. The media in
industrial disputes, or in political demonstrations, can have the
effect either of exacerbating or restraining violence. There are
examples of both of these effects in Chapters 2 and 3. If reporting
seems to be biased or misleading it can cause great resentment. A
dispute, or the media coverage of it, can again be exploited with
the specific aim of discrediting the police.

The third form of political violence – terrorism – is of an
entirely different nature. During the past ten years, over 2000
people have been killed by terrorists in Northern Ireland. In
Chapter 9 we examine the problems of the media operating in a
community containing rival violent factions, each of which considers that 'he who is not with us is against us', and the professionalism with which one of these factions, the Provisional IRA,
uses the media in what amounts to a propaganda war supported by
a shooting war. In Chapter 10 we look at the problems of a government and of its police and army press offices in fighting such a war,
and how this can provide lessons for other large public or private
organizations in dealing with the media in a conflict situation.

Of approximately 75 terrorist murders in Britain itself during
the period 1972–80, none have been by indigenous British terrorists. Sixty-one were killed by members of Irish terrorist movements, and the remainder by Arab terrorists. None of the victims
of the latter have been British; all have been Arabs, Iranians or
Israelis temporarily visiting or working in Britain. These terrorist
murders have thus not had their roots in British society at all.
Apart from the Northern Ireland studies in Chapters 9 and 10 the
study of the influence of the British media on terrorism is directed
to the ethics of giving access for publicity to terrorist movements
and to the possibility of placing lives at risk in reporting kidnapping and hostage situations (Chapters 11 to 13).

A very large number of books has been written in recent years
about the media and a selection of these is listed, each with a brief
outline of its approach, in the Bibliography at the back of the
book.

They include some excellent books on how newspapers are controlled and produced and on how news is gathered, of which the
best are Steve Chibnall's *Law and Order News*, Simon Jenkins's

Newspapers: The Power and the Money, Chapman Pincher's *Inside Story* and John Whale's *The Politics of the Media.* All of the authors are professional journalists.

Equally professional in the field of television news production are Ivor Yorke's *The Technique of Television News* and the BBC's own monograph *The Task of Broadcasting News.* For an outside point of view see *Putting 'Reality' Together: BBC News* by Philip Schlesinger, a sociologist PhD student who was given access by the BBC as a 'fly on the wall'.

For the layman, the most lucid and readable account covering all the media is Alan Hooper's *The Military and the Media.* He deals with the press, radio and television, including news, documentaries and drama, and discusses how a large organization (in this case the armed forces) can best work with them. Denis Mac-Shane, in *Using the Media,* also describes in detail how newspapers and programmes are produced and advises trade unionists and individual workers (e.g. pickets) on how best to use them – advice which is also given less comprehensively in the TUC pamphlet, *How to Handle the Media.*

The media coverage of industrial disputes is well analyzed in the BBC's *Coverage of the Industrial Situation in January and February 1979* and IBA's *Television Coverage of Industrial Conflict.* The TUC criticizes this coverage in *A Cause for Concern.* The special problems of the media in dealing with terrorism are covered in the Institute for the Study of Conflict's *Television and Conflict,* and in two journals – in a complete issue of Yonah Alexander's *Terrorism, an International Journal* and in an article by Walter Jaehnig, 'Journalists and Terrorism' in the *Indiana Law Journal.*

There is a mass of books about bias or political motivation of the media and this aspect is mentioned in many of the above, notably MacShane's *Using the Media.* Less partisan is Michael Tracey's *The Production of Political Television.* Robin Day's argument in *Day by Day* – that television 'should sustain the Reasonable Society together with its parliamentary institutions' – has already been mentioned. By contrast Robert Hargreaves, formerly ITN's Home Affairs Correspondent, in an article in M. J. Clark (ed.) *Politics and the Media,* argues that television should show no bias towards existing social mores, though he does quote ITN's former Editor, Sir Geoffrey Cox, as supporting Robin Day's approach. Lord Windlesham, Chairman of ATV, also argues against government

interference, while accepting the need for broadcasters to show
responsibility, in *Broadcasting in a Free Society*. Varying views are
reported by Robin Walsh, Martin Bell and others in an interesting
seminar on 'Terrorism and the Media' recorded in the Royal
United Services Institute's *Ten Years of Terrorism*. The Glasgow
Media Group, in *Bad News* and *More Bad News* accuse both ITN
and BBC News of bias towards the government's line and against
the trade unions. The leader of the group, Peter Beharrell, with
Greg Philo, in *Trade Unions and the Media* takes a more openly
political line in ascribing this bias to the small group of owners and
managers of the media.

In an interesting foreword to *Bad News*, Dr Richard Hoggart
refers to what he calls the 'low conspiracy' and 'high conspiracy'
theories of control of the media. The 'low conspiracy theory' envisages direct pressure on editors and journalists by, for example,
informal telephone calls or personal approaches from government
ministers, employers or others acting on their behalf. The 'high
conspiracy theory' envisages a much less direct approach by more
hidden forces, such as selective recruitment and encouragement of
the belief that failure to observe certain political and social mores
will be detrimental to career prospects, so that no direct pressure
is needed. Hoggart rightly dismisses both of these theories as
simplistic.

In practice, the prime motivation of most journalists is to attract
an audience. This is not only for the obvious reasons inherent in
a commercial organization because it applies just as much to
journalists (and authors, producers, etc.) in the BBC as it does to
ITV and the press. This motivation arises from the almost
universal human desire to get a response — to be appreciated —
and from professional pride. The Editor of *The Sun* clearly took
pride in overhauling the circulation of the *Mirror* and the *Express*
and no doubt had a conscious policy of printing stories which
would not only strike a chord with his own regular readers but
would also attract readers from his rivals. If journalists send their
editor stories which contribute to this aim, they will obviously
enhance their prospects for promotion and for interesting assignments. Similarly, if one of the BBC producers in the *Panorama*
team always increased the audience ratings when his programmes
came on he could expect better and better opportunities; if, however, he drove the viewers away he could expect soon to be dropped
from *Panorama* and to get more and more dismal assignments.

The motivation is professional rather than commercial, and, for most journalists, their personal political views enter into it very little.

This motivation does not necessarily make for honest or accurate journalism. When the author visited Vietnam in 1967 he was staggered by the lack of resemblance between what he saw and what he had been reading for the previous five years in the press. On his return to Singapore he invited three journalist friends to supper and indicted them: 'Your reporting is like a photograph from a satellite when the world is covered with cloud at 10 000 feet. All you record are the jagged peaks which bear no relation to the real world in the inhabited valleys.' They counter-attacked: 'We report what you want to read. If we sent our editor stuff which would bore the readers he would not print it. If we went on doing so he would replace us with someone who sent him stuff he could use — the peaks. You buy the papers; blame yourself, not us.'

So, as we shall see in the case-studies in this book, the media magnify the violent picket, the violent demonstrator and the terrorist; they magnify the corrupt policeman; and they are sometimes unscrupulous in exacerbating the violence and even risking lives in order to get reports of good news value. They can do this from political motives but much more often their motives are professional. The result is part of the nature of the media in a free society. The problem is that the alternative, media under state control or censorship, is far worse, and a sure road to oppressive government.

After the case-studies in Parts I, II and III, Part IV of this book draws some conclusions on how best to live with the media as they are, either as individuals or as representatives of public or private organizations. The final chapter examines what editors and journalists themselves can do to alleviate the damage which the media can do in a conflict situation: when, for example, they needlessly exacerbate the conflict or arouse violence; or when they knowingly or recklessly put lives at risk by hampering the rescue of hostages. Should these abuses of the power of the media be subject to statutory restraint by legislation, or to voluntary control by their own professional institutions, or is it enough to leave this to the integrity and good sense of journalists? These are some of the questions which must be faced by the media in a reasonable society if it is to remain reasonable.

Part I
Industrial Disputes

1   A Bias against the Unions?

PEACEFUL PICKETING

No one has been killed on a picket line in Great Britain since 1911, other than in traffic accidents. This is all the more remarkable in view of the intensity of the bitterness between strikers and non-strikers. The striker regards the 'scab' who goes to work as a traitor who undermines the strike, continues to draw his pay and, worst of all, takes the benefit from any settlement for higher wages without sharing in the sacrifice. The non-striker, for his part, resents the coercion and the intimidation, physical or psychological, and resents being made to feel guilty because of his beliefs; he resents it all the more when his main concern is for his family or the community (particularly if he is a public service worker) rather than for himself.

Yet actual violence between strikers and non-strikers has been rare in Britain. This is partly because the pickets are in an organized body supporting each other whereas the man trying to go to work does so as an individual and is unlikely to pick a fight with a dozen hostile pickets, still less with a mass picket. Violence would probably occur more often if the non-strikers went to work in organized bodies for mutual protection.

There is much more violence between pickets and police, because the police on picket lines *are* an organized body, with a legal obligation to take positive action to prevent assault, intimidation and obstruction, if possible by persuasion but if necessary by physically preventing it or by arresting offenders. This can be exploited. As one shop steward put it to the author, one of his problems was to get his people 'involved in the struggle' and for this it may be necessary to arouse hatred. 'My lads regard the police as their friends. I have to convince them that they are enemies. There's nothing like a bit of violence to do that, provided that they blame the police and not me for starting it.'[1]

13

THE ATTITUDES AND EFFECTS OF THE MEDIA

The media both encourage and discourage violent picketing. The fact that violence is news may encourage some militant leaders to use it, or at least to arouse the media's expectation of it, in order to attract attention. On the other hand, they know that violence is unpopular with the public, and they may therefore restrain their firebrands in front of the cameras for fear of losing public sympathy. The media had both of these effects at various times at Grunwick in 1977, as will be discussed in Chapter 3.

Another influence of the media on industrial disputes is that most trade unionists believe, rightly or wrongly, that the media are prejudiced against them. The TUC have published a pamphlet, *A Cause for Concern*,[2] which aims to prove their bias by quotations from the coverage of the disputes in January and February 1979; at the same time they issued a pamphlet called *How to Handle the Media: A Guide for Trade Unionists*.[3]

A more political viewpoint is apparent in *Trade Unions and the Media* ('The common interest of the contributors here is in how the organization of the media, and what it produces, reflects the power of dominant interests in society at large'). The editors of that book also draw attention to the imbalance between the treatment of strikes and low investment as causes of poor industrial performance.

> We are regularly informed, for example, of how much lost production is being 'caused' by the strike. We also know who is to 'blame' for this problem . . . . There is no critical account, let alone routine referencing, of problems such as the export of private capital, or the movement of capital away from productive industry into various forms of profiteering such as speculation in land or commodities.[4]

This problem of providing better background information in television coverage of industrial disputes is discussed in Chapter 4.

Denis MacShane, 1978—9 President of the NUJ, declares his political hand more explicitly on the first page of his book *Using the Media*. 'The British mass media is firmly locked into (or in the BBC's case linked to) British capitalism . . . . At key moments the whole weight of the mass media can be thrown against working people . . .'[5] He seems to envisage something even more direct than the 'low conspiracy' or 'high conspiracy' theories noted and rejected by Richard Hoggart in his foreward to *Bad News*.[6] 'At key moments the whole weight of the mass media can be thrown . . .' conjures up a picture of a Minister of Information closeted with newspaper and television editors planning an orchestrated presentation of doctored news as in the Soviet Union or Nazi Germany. As a former *Daily Mirror* and BBC journalist he knows well enough how the British media work, and he is writing a political book. It is, however, the trade union activists who organize and man the picket lines; many of these, not having MacShane's knowledge of the media, will accept his views and will communicate them to their members, who become frustrated by the feeling that the media are not giving them fair treatment. The media and especially the popular press and TV news, do tend to reflect what their editors perceive to be the views of the majority of their readers and viewers, as is discussed more fully later. There is nothing inherently evil in this unless they knowingly reinforce false prejudices or inflame people to violence. The media should certainly not report something which they know to be untrue just because they think that their readers will like it. About 75 per cent of viewers of BBC News and nearer 90 per cent of ITN viewers are manual workers.[7] MacShane's contention is that the editors choose what to tell them not because they will necessarily like it but because it is what 'British capitalism' believes will be good for them to hear in order to preserve the *status quo*. The essential question is whether the news and comment on industrial disputes is accurately, honestly and fairly presented. This question is examined more fully in Chapter 4, and there are examples which can be quoted to support either contention. When editors present news with a calculated political bias they can fairly be described as political activists. Another kind of political activist, however, may wish to advance his aims by exacerbating industrial conflict. A good way to do this is to ensure that, whether the media coverage is fair or unfair, people on picket lines *believe* it to be unfair, because this leads to frustration, frustration leads to violence and violence gets people 'involved in the struggle'.

PUBLIC DISLIKE OF STRIKES

Regardless of any political bias either in MacShane's thesis or

amongst newspaper and programme editors, the media do undoubtedly reflect the popular dislike of strikes and strikers and the
consequent unpopularity of the trade unions. Most big institutions
are unpopular and the more the public sees them as a harassment
the more unpopular they are. Conversely, if their workers are seen
primarily as providing an essential service and still more so if they
are facing danger or hardship on behalf of the public they are
treated more sympathetically. Amongst those traditionally en-
joying such sympathy have been firemen, ambulance drivers,
doctors, nurses, miners and soldiers and also the police, in whose
case the 'service' and 'danger' image significantly outweighs the
'harassment' image. As soon as any public service workers go on
strike, however, the 'harassment' image takes over. Soldiers and
policemen cannot strike. In 1972 the miners, who had not had a
national strike since 1926, enjoyed majority public support at the
start of their strike but had lost it within a few weeks, largely due to
the violence at the Saltley Coke Depot. Since flying pickets and
mass pickets at that time were both relatively new, this received a
good deal of coverage on the media (see next chapter). Within two
years they called another national strike, this time coinciding with
the quadrupling of oil prices in January 1974, resulting in much
public suffering. Although this strike brought down the Heath
Government, the public have never since felt the same about the
miners. A public opinion poll in November 1977 showed that 75
per cent of the people were prepared to 'endure a miserable winter
of strikes and power cuts rather than give the miners preference
over other workers'.[8] The firemen did the same to themselves in
1977 and the ambulance men in 1979. All achieved large pay rises,
but in the long run their sacrifice of public sympathy may more
than outweigh their gain and this will add to their bitterness in
future disputes.

For other workers, without the 'danger' or 'hardship' image, the
threshold of public exasperation is lower. It is a natural human
failing to condemn other people's demands for higher wages but not
one's own. Everyone, whether a 'dirty job' man or a craftsman or a
managing director, feels that his own job is undervalued and that his
pay should catch up with that of others — certainly not the other way
round. When there is a strike, therefore, most of the public dislike it,
some because they resent the strikers trying to steal a march over pay
by virtue of the degree of disruption they can cause, and others
because of the effects of this disruption on their own lives.

ATTRACTING READERS AND VIEWERS

It was argued in the Introduction that, in a country where the media have editorial freedom, editors and journalists are primarily motivated by a desire to sound a responsive chord amongst their regular readers and amongst those most likely to be attracted away from a rival paper or programme; that this applies equally to the BBC as to commercial television or newspapers, because it is a symptom of editorial freedom rather than pure commercialism; that it applies as much to junior reporters as to senior editors, since advancement and opportunities go to those whose work is seen as attracting rather than repelling readers and viewers. With all its faults (ambition, ruthless competitiveness, envy, greed) this is a healthier motive than that in a country where the media are controlled by the state, where the advancement of opportunities open to a journalist depend, not upon his attracting readers and viewers, but on his ability to persuade them to believe what the government wishes them to believe. The same might apply if the media were a monopoly, either of one giant corporation or of a single trade union such as the NUJ, if it were able to compel all editors to be members of a closed shop, subject to dismissal if they were judged to have acted 'contrary to the interests of the union', but this will not apply so long as the media compete with each other.

The motivation of editors to attract readers is illustrated by the coverage of any major strike in the *Sun*, the *Daily Express* and the *Daily Mirror*. All three are read predominantly by manual workers: respectively 77 per cent, 55 per cent and 75 per cent of their readership. Put another way, 87 per cent of all manual workers in Britain read one of these three papers, and of these 52 per cent read the *Sun* or the *Express* and 35 per cent read the *Mirror*.[9] The majority of those who read the *Sun* and the *Express* will probably disagree with most strikes, and this is reflected editorially. Where their readers have sympathy (e.g. for miners) the paper too will reflect that sympathy. Though the TUC pamphlet complains about this,[10] most readers of most papers understand it perfectly well, and will be in no way ashamed of buying the paper which reflects their own views. The *Mirror* openly declares this philosophy in the title under which (though currently second in circulation to the *Sun*) it has sold far more copies over the past 30 years than any other paper. Since the sector of the public whose views it aims primarily to mirror are those manual workers who vote Labour, it will often take up the case for a strike, particularly if there is a case for blaming Tory policy for it. MacShane points out that the *Mirror*'s parent company, IPC, has wide business interests which would be best served by a Tory Government and a strike-free society but this fact has little influence on editorial policy. IPC's capitalist interest lies primarily in the *Mirror* attracting and retaining its own sector of the public as readers. When the *Mirror* does oppose a strike (e.g. the transport and public service strike in January 1979[11]) it is because its editor judges that this does mirror the views of most of its readers.

The only papers with a national circulation which will almost invariably support a strike are the Communist *Morning Star* (circulation 22 000) and the Trotskyist *Socialist Worker* (peak circulation in 1974 was 30 000),[12] whose readerships are tiny compared with those of the national daily and Sunday papers. They again mirror their readers' views because they are unlikely to be read by many people who do not themselves support most strikes as part of a political war to cause the collapse of the capitalist society.

THE BITTERNESS OF BEING REJECTED

The frustrating fact for trade unionists today, however, is that the chief sufferers in almost every industrial dispute are members of the public who see no compensating benefit for themselves from any strike. This applies not only to strikes of publicly owned services and industries, which make up by far the largest number of lost working days, but also to most strikes in private firms because of the increasing complexity and interdependence of industry. A strike in a component factory will probably cause many more layoffs elsewhere than the number of strikers, not to mention the irritation caused to members of the public awaiting delivery of products using these components. The trade union concerned, and often the TUC, will plead that 'our fight is your fight — for better wages for all workers' but the reader or viewer knows well enough that a rise for all is a rise for none, and that real gains come only to those with the muscle to demand — and get — a bigger rise than others. The 'others', even those who do not suffer directly from the strike, can hardly be expected to sympathize very often. So it is axiomatic that, first, the majority will seldom sympathize with the strikers, secondly, the media reflect that view and thirdly, the strikers conclude that the media are 'hostile'. For those strikers who recognize that this hostility is logical and does in fact reflect popular feeling, it merely increases the frustration and bitterness. The exploitation of this frustration and bitterness is a boon to those of the strike leaders who believe that the explosion of the strike into violence will further their aims, by gaining publicity or by getting more of their apathetic members 'involved in the struggle' or, on a wider field, provoking an overreaction which will erode the general public support for the police.

This effect of the media in developing the bitterness and frustration, whether by hostility or indifference to the strike, or by publishing news which was in itself unintentionally inflammatory, will be examined in the contexts of the incident at the Saltley Coke Depot, the 1976–7 dispute at the Grunwick factory and the transport and public service strikes of January–February 1979.

2 The Battle of Saltley, 1972

THE 1972 MINERS' STRIKE

The 1972 miners' strike caused a remarkable change in public attitude towards the miners. When it began in January over 50 per cent of the public sympathized with their demand for a pay rise substantially higher than that for other workers, which was restricted by government to a norm of 8 per cent. When it ended on 25 February the miners had achieved a rise of 27 per cent, but by then the public feeling had swung heavily against them and has remained so.[1] This swing in public opinion followed the wide publicity given to the violence on the picket line at the Saltley Coke Depot, on the outskirts of Birmingham, between 5 and 10 February 1972.

The media had played a role beneficial to the miners during the previous years. Throughout the 1960s, while Lord Robens[2] was Chairman of the National Coal Board (NCB), cheap oil had caused a steady retrenchment in the coal industry, resulting in the closure of 400 pits and the loss of 400 000 jobs. Robens had persuaded the miners that if wages rose too high many more pits would become uneconomical, particularly the older pits in areas where there was no alternative employment, such as South Wales and the North East. This would have meant the destruction and dispersal of tightly-knit mining communities. Robens was a strong and much respected leader and enjoyed an 'adversary partnership' with an equally strong President of the National Union of Mineworkers (NUM), Will Paynter. Under their leadership the miners, by tradition a united and mutually compassionate community, accepted a decline in their position in the wages league table rather than cause greater suffering for their brothers in what would have become dead towns before alternative industries could be developed.[3] Their forbearance did not go unnoticed by the media. The public, who had no illusions about the hardships and dangers faced by the miners, were sympathetic with their case for climbing back to their position as the best paid of manual workers.

At the end of 1970, just after the miners had accepted a relatively moderate pay rise,[4] the electric power workers staged a 'go-slow' which led to a State of Emergency and won a rise of 15 per cent.[5] In 1971, just as the NUM were preparing a 40 per cent demand to catch up their lost ground, the government placed an 8 per cent ceiling on all wage rises. The fury of the miners, who were no longer under the strong Robens/Paynter leadership, could not be contained and the first national miners' strike for 46 years began in an atmosphere of frustration and bitter determination – and initially, with a great deal of public sympathy. The media had bred this sympathy, not only over the years of restraint, but also by contrasting the treatment of the miners and that of the power workers, who had a relatively safe job and had alienated themselves from the public who had suffered from the power cuts by which they had extracted their pay rise.

ARTHUR SCARGILL'S OPERATIONS ROOM

The miners, from the start, began what would now be called secondary picketing – particularly of ports and power stations. Some of their picket organizers also took a positive attitude to using the media. One BBC producer with an outside broadcast unit noticed that his team always seemed to be expected when it arrived at a picketed gate, and that the pickets were ready to put on a performance for it. He then noticed that wherever they were filming there seemed to be a couple of strikers hovering in the vicinity of their van, listening to the radio chat with BBC headquarters. When this indicated a move to a new location, he saw the eavesdroppers go off to a telephone box, watching and reporting the progress of the team in packing up and presumably forecasting its time of arrival at the next site.[6]

The media also played a major part in bringing about the incident which caused the strike to explode into violence. On 3 February 1972 the *Birmingham Mail* ran a story about a traffic jam a mile long as 'lorries from all over the country waited at Saltley, Britain's last major gas coke stockpile'. The national press and television took up the story, with photographs of the lorry queues with the 'mountain of coke' in the background, from which the Gas Board admitted that 30 000 tons had been collected since the strike began.

The Staffordshire miners put a picket on the coke depot, but the police restricted it to 16 men and the lorries, mainly driven by non-union self-employed drivers, took little notice. A normal flow of 400 lorries a day had risen to 600–700 and there were reports of scuffles on the picket line. The miners were angry at what they saw as a leakage nullifying the effects of their stoppage of coal from the pit-head stocks, and this led to a ready response to the call for rein-forcement by flying pickets from Yorkshire.

The flying pickets were efficiently organized by Arthur Scargill, who had already been using them around the ports and power stations of Yorkshire and East Anglia. In his office in Barnsley was what can only be described as a 'war room'. On the wall was an operations map showing every colliery, power station, port and steelworks. On the table was a log book showing the number of pickets available at operational readiness at each colliery, together with the telephone numbers of coach firms which, in exchange for a retainer fee, had undertaken to provide coaches at immediate notice to transport the flying pickets. Arthur Scargill received the call from Birmingham at 4 p.m. on Saturday 5 February, with no prior warning. Within three hours he had 200 pickets on the road with another 200 following soon after – no small achievement on a Saturday afternoon at the peak of the football season.[7]

THE BATTLE OF SALTLEY

As well as being a superb organizer, Scargill knew how to capture the attention of the media. For five days 'The Battle of Saltley' dominated the news bulletins. Other NUM areas sent contingents, and the era of the 'mass picket' was born, with 2000 pickets heaving at a cordon of 800 police as some 40 lorries, one by one, were brought through to the gate each day. Just as the Wembley crowd puts a football team on its mettle, so the presence of the cameras and the nightly replay of the day's events on television aroused the passion and determination of the miners.

The attention of the motor workers and others in Birmingham factories had also been attracted by the reports of the battle on their doorstep. At the end of the second day of mass picketing (Tuesday 8 February) Arthur Scargill made an emotional appeal to a special district meeting of the Amalgamated Union of Engineering Workers (AUEW) and called for a massive sympathy strike on Thursday 10 February. Representatives of the Transport and General Workers' Union (TGWU) were also at the meeting and promised their support. On the Thursday morning, the 800 police cordoning Nechells Place — the funnel-shaped entrance to the coke depot gate from the main Saltley Road — were engulfed, like 'the jam in a layer-cake'[8] by a crowd of 15 000, totally blocking both Nechells Place and the main road. As things stood no lorries were able to get anywhere near Nechells Place and the Chief Constable, Sir Derrick Capper, considered that not only was it pointless to maintain the cordon but that there would be a risk of death or serious injury if the police were to try to force a passage. At 11 a.m. he requested the Depot Manager to close the gates and announced that they would remain closed for the rest of the day. The gates were physically closed by a senior police officer in front of the television cameras so the incident was made into a symbolic public surrender of the police to the power of the mass pickets. The Chief Constable then asked Arthur Scargill to disperse the crowd, and handed him the police microphone with which to do it. Scargill gave a political speech claiming, in his own words, 'living proof that the working class had only to flex its muscles and it could bring Government, employers, society to a total standstill'.[9]

Scargill's victory was complete and with it came victory for the miners as a whole. They ended the strike on 25 February with a 27 per cent rise and by the autumn the national wage rises were averaging 15 to 17 per cent. The government's attempt to hold an 8 per cent ceiling had collapsed.

Sir Derrick Capper was widely criticized for closing the gates, particularly by Conservative MPs and by some other policemen. He did, however, demonstrate beyond doubt the independence of a British Chief Constable from the government, and his right to interpret the law with discretion. He was not a man who sought publicity but he had appeared briefly with Arthur Scargill on a local television programme while the confrontation was in progress. Though he did not say much in front of the camera he had a conversation with Scargill before the programme and told him that, if the Saltley Coke Depot were forced to close he would resign. In the event, he retired in 1974, his health broken, and he died soon afterwards. In an interview with the author just before he retired, he said that he would never know whether his decision was right or wrong but that he was convinced on 10 February that unless the crowd was dispersed there was a serious risk of heavy bloodshed in a situation which he could no longer control.

With hindsight, it might be argued that he need only have closed the depot for that day. It was not until the afternoon that it was agreed between the police, the NUM and the Depot Manager that all loading would cease, not just for the day, but until the end of the strike, except for those lorries carrying union permits to collect coke for essential services such as hospitals, schools and for distribution to old people. The Chief Constable felt that, without such an agreement, the mass picket would be renewed indefinitely now that it had proved effective, with further publicity and further exacerbation of the violence. The events at Grunwick five years later suggests that his prognosis may have been right but that the decision itself may have been wrong.

In many countries the police would have blasted a way through the crowd with water cannon and tear gas but this was never seriously considered. Arthur Scargill, in an interview with the author in 1976, said that if this had been done, violence would have exploded on picket lines all over the country. But would not this, he was asked, have suited him, as a Marxist, in creating a revolutionary situation? He replied that, if his leadership had resulted in the media being saturated with scenes of violence, with hundreds of miners, other workers and police being killed or injured, his men would have blamed him for starting it and he would have lost their support. In this opinion he was probably sincere and probably right.

THE INFLUENCE OF THE MEDIA

As it was, the nightly television drama of Saltley had alarmed the public, and so had the spectacle of public surrender by the police to mob rule under an avowedly revolutionary leader. Nevertheless, the violence did not compare in intensity or viciousness with that at Grunwick in 1977. Thirty people were injured at Saltley, of whom 16 were police. One senior police officer was seriously injured, not deliberately with a milk bottle, as at Grunwick (see next chapter) but accidentally when the cordon was pushed over into the path of a lorry. This incident itself revealed the absence of real hatred at

Saltley, for the miners at once suspended hostilities and co-operated with the police in the task of getting an ambulance in and the injured man out as quickly as possible. This would not have happened at Grunwick where, except on one day, the majority of the 'pickets' were student demonstrators. At Saltley they were virtually all miners until they were joined by other trade unionists in the one-day strike on 10 February. Of 76 pickets arrested at Saltley, 61 were miners, nine other workers and only six students or academics.

Nevertheless, mild as the Saltley violence now appears, the public reaction to it at the time alarmed the trade unions. Two years later, in the strikes which brought down the Heath Government all the unions concerned (NUM, NUR, ASLEF, TGWU and GMWU) went to great lengths to restrict their pickets to six men and to avoid violence at all costs. A major factor here, of course, was that the public regarded the trade unions as almost synonymous with the Labour Party, so both Mr Wilson and the TUC were well aware that any repetition of Saltley could cost Labour the election. This, however, merely underlines the depth of the public reaction to the Saltley drama, and the concern in the Labour Party and the unions at how deep it was.

To summarize the influence of the media in this instance: the long-term coverage of the miners' restraint over the past decade had built an undercurrent of public sympathy which was reinforced when the power station workers, unpopular after a winter of power cuts, stole a march on them in the Wilberforce settlement. This had itself received detailed background coverage in the media. The miners' strike developed the techniques of secondary picketing and of flying pickets, and in some cases the pickets made calculated use of the media, especially of television, by orchestrating their action so as to provide 'good television' pictures when the cameras were there. The incident at Saltley, and the passions it aroused, were a direct consequence of press and television pictures of the queues of lorries drawing from the 'mountain of coke' to undermine the strike. This passion led to violence and the public triumph of what its leader proclaimed as the irresistible revolutionary force of the crowd. This worried the public and had two major effects: the forfeiture of public sympathy for the miners, which appears to be long-lasting and possibly even permanent; and a determination by the trade unions to avoid similar incidents, a determination which was successfully maintained until Grunwick in 1977, the 'Winter of Discontent' in 1979 and the steel strike in 1980.

The other major effect of the media coverage of Saltley was the overnight creation of Arthur Scargill as a public figure. Aged 34 at the time, he emerged from an unglamorous appointment in the Barnsley NUM office as a folk hero, and was soon afterwards elected President of the Yorkshire Area of the NUM. Since then he has never looked back, and arouses passionate emotions on all sides. He delights in being seen by the Establishment as the devil incarnate. His own Yorkshire miners follow him because he gets them the benefits they want; and he is one of the rare people who attract the allegiance of the whole of the far left, from the left wing of the Labour Party and the Communist Party, to the student Trotskyist movements and the London *radical chic*.

He knows what he owes to the media and he cultivates his image with an engaging sense of humour. When the NUM provided him with a Volvo car this attracted much adverse publicity. He tackled it head on, as he does with other criticisms. A newspaper profile quoted a favourite story: 'Arthur Scargill and Joe Gormley go to heaven. St Peter promises to keep Scargill out of Gormley's hair. One day a Volvo whizzes past Gormley's cloud and knocks him off. Gormley expostulates to St Peter who says: "Oh, that wasn't Arthur Scargill. That was God. He just *thinks* he's Arthur Scargill."'[10]

3 Grunwick

A FRONT-PAGE STORM IN A TEACUP

'Never, in the reporting of industrial conflict have so many heard so much about so few.' The Grunwick strike provides an example of how a small conflict may be exploited to obtain publicity for wider causes. This was done by both sides, one with skill and the other with a series of errors which led to the total failure of the strike.

The dispute lasted nearly two years. It concerned a factory which, at the peak of the dispute, employed only 270 workers and there were 91 others on strike, all of whom had been sacked. The number of official pickets seldom exceeded 12. Yet this tiny dispute formed a focus for pressure groups of the far right and the far left, politicians from right, left and centre, and above all, a mass demonstration of between 700 and 2000 students for two weeks, rising on one occasion to 18 000.

In contrast to Saltley, where the mass picket (until the last day) consisted mainly of 2000 miners on strike, there was never a mass picket at Grunwick, nor did the small official picket of strikers use violence against the police or against those going to work. The students around the gates were not on strike, and were not regarded as pickets by most of the strikers, nor by the Labour Government of the day. They were demonstrators in the vicinity of a picket, and very violent ones — much more violent than the miners at Saltley as the figures show: [1]

	Saltley 1972	Grunwick 1977
Duration of mass action	5 days	28 days
Largest number of pickets	2 000	12
Largest number of demonstrators	15 000 (10 Feb)	18 000 (11 July)
Largest number of police	800 (10 Feb)	3 500 (11 July)
Number of arrests	61	377
Number of police injured	16	243

The media played a major part in the Grunwick dispute. For the first 10 months, it was virtually ignored and this proved extremely frustrating to the dozen or so pickets who stood stolidly at the gate, ignored as much by the non-strikers as the press. After an abortive attempt by three government ministers to attract attention by joining the pickets, the mass demonstration was called and during the next four weeks Grunwick was front page news and all the injuries were caused. Finally, after a prolonged series of hearings in the High Court, Court of Appeal and House of Lords, and an inquiry by Lord Scarman, the strike petered out over the next 12 months and ended with none of its aims achieved and none of the strikers getting their jobs back.

The Grunwick factory (or group of factories) was located in a run-down area of Willesden in North West London, with a high immigrant population. Three-quarters of the Grunwick workers were Gujerati-speaking Indians, with a high percentage of women, who knew that they had little chance of getting any other job in the area, or even (if they were married, as many of them were) of drawing the dole.

The proprietor, George Ward, was himself an immigrant, half Indian, who had created Grunwick from nothing in 12 years and had become a rich man. It had by 1976 become a highly successful mail order film-processing laboratory, and was named by the consumer magazine *Which* as the fastest firm in the business, beating the giants like Kodak both in speed and prices. To achieve this, Ward worked very hard himself and only employed workers who agreed to accept compulsory overtime without holidays during the peak 'holiday snap' months of July, August and September. He was clearly determined not to allow trade unions to prejudice his efficiency in this highly competitive market. Various attempts to form a union branch had failed and Grunwick remained a non-union firm. The 91 workers who went on strike were not union members but they joined a union after they walked out. The dispute was about the recognition of this union by the firm.

Around this small dispute huge institutions and interest groups brought their weight to bear. It was the first serious test of the government's Employment Protection Act (EPA) which came into force in 1976, under which the Advisory, Conciliation and Arbitration Service (ACAS) was responsible for resolving recognition disputes. The union concerned — The Association of Professional, Executive and Computer Staff (APEX) — fully involved themselves and so, to their subsequent regret, did three ministers who were APEX-sponsored MPs. Later, eight Tribune Group MPs also joined in, along with Arthur Scargill and Mick McGahey of the NUM. As the *Sunday Times* Insight Team remarked: 'The whole panoply of the left, from International Marxists to Gay Liberationists, parades daily. "This is the Ascot of the left" one said. "It is essential to be seen here, best of all to get arrested".'[2]

TEN MONTHS OF FRUSTRATION

The dispute began in August 1976[3] during the peak season for film processing in a very hot summer. After a relatively minor quarrel between a manager and about half a dozen workers over getting some work finished in time to catch the post, 91 regular and 46 temporary staff (mainly students with vacation jobs) walked out. None of the 91 were members of a trade union but they consulted the Brent Trades Council whose secretary, Jack Dromey, advised them to join APEX. Dromey and the APEX area organizer helped them to form a strike committee.

On 1 September APEX, claiming recognition as a union under the EPA, made the strike official. Next day Ward sacked all the 137 strikers for breach of contract — which was lawful provided that he sacked them all and did not discriminate. The other workers had no wish to join the strike and ignored the small picket on the gate led by a tiny Indian woman, Mrs Desai, who had been one of those involved in the original shopfloor quarrel.

Grunwick declined the request for recognition so APEX appealed for conciliation to ACAS, who proposed a ballot of strikers and non-strikers, and asked George Ward to provide the names and addresses of those still working in the factory. Ward repeatedly declined this request. The Union of Postal Workers (UPW) thereupon blacked Grunwick's mail which, for a mail order firm, could quickly have led to its bankruptcy. At this, the National Association for Freedom (NAFF) threw its weight behind Ward, offering the services of their solicitors to seek a High Court Order to the Post Office to resume deliveries under the Post Office Act of 1969. The UPW, knowing that they would lose the case and that, in any case, blacking of mail aroused powerful public emotions, called off their boycott.

This was on 5 November 1976 and did attract some attention in the press. Thereafter, however, interest waned as the wrangling between Grunwick, ACAS and APEX over recognition continued and the picket of Indian women, with a few English supporters, stood forlorn and shivering at the gates through the winter months. By May 1977 they were losing heart.

At this stage Roy Grantham, the General Secretary of APEX, decided to make a positive effort to attract the attention of the media to their struggle, and called upon four MPs sponsored by APEX to appear with him on the picket line in the last week of May. Three of them were government ministers — Shirley Williams, Fred Mulley and Denis Howell. They certainly did attract the attention of the media.[4] In view of the violence which followed three weeks later they probably regretted it, because their names became associated with that violence. This was unjust because their aim, as well-known Labour moderates, was undoubtedly to make a final attempt to help Roy Grantham's impeccably lawful, patient and constitutional campaign to succeed — in the hope of heading off the militancy and violence which seemed otherwise almost certain to explode.

They got the publicity but Ward and NAFF did not budge. At this point, moderation having failed, the left took over. The bridge was Mrs Desai's strike committee adviser, Jack Dromey, who was a member of the Tribune Group and 1976 Chairman of the National Council for Civil Liberties (NCCL). Up till then he had gone along with Grantham's moderation but at the end of May he published a call for a mass picket on 13 June — the first mass picket since Saltley. Grantham agreed, not without some misgivings, that this was the only way to attract public attention.

The far left eagerly took up the call. The CPGB *Morning Star* came out in support but the lead was quickly taken over by the Socialist Workers' Party (SWP), a Trotskyist movement, the largest section of whose 5000 members were graduates or university students, most of whom would by 13 June have finished their examinations. From 23 May onwards the SWP newspaper, *Socialist Worker*, called upon them to be at Grunwick on that day and daily thereafter. In the first 10 days of June SWP issued 22 000 leaflets and put up 2000 wall posters in London. They said that if the numbers were big enough the police would not dare to provoke a confrontation and that 'aggressive picketing can close the factory'.[5]

THE VIOLENCE BEGINS

The national press and television became interested, with the promise of a confrontation, and on 13 June reporters and cameras were ready at the Grunwick gate, which is on a narrow bend in a residential road just outside Dollis Hill underground station. This enabled London University students in particular to be there without difficulty by the time the gates opened and to be back in central London by 9 a.m. if they wished. Television producers made 'facility agreements' to rent first-floor rooms with windows overlooking the gate.

It was a Monday morning and Mrs Desai and her faithful pickets were joined initially by 200 later increasing to 700 demonstrators who attempted to form a physical block across the gates. The police, who had been formally notified by APEX that there was to be a mass picket, warned the demonstrators that they were unlawfully obstructing the public highway. When they did not move, the police formed a cordon to open access for those waiting to go to work. Violence broke out almost at once and 84 demonstrators, most of them students, were arrested.

Probably as a consequence of the build-up of the mass picket in the *Morning Star* and *Socialist Worker*, or perhaps in coordination with it, a number of left-wing Labour MPs visited the pickets during the morning – and raised the matter in Parliament the same afternoon, accusing the police of 'unnecessary brutality' and 'aggressive and provocative tactics'. Merlyn Rees (Home Secretary) and other ministers, however, blamed the demonstrators and expressed support for the police. Superintendent Hickman-Smith, who was in charge on the day, was interviewed by reporters on the site and his comments were repeated the same evening on television and next morning in the press:

> Everyone who wanted to go into work was being called a 'scab' and shouted at. There were about 200 people massing outside the gates and we had to put a cordon on to allow free access to the premises. I do not think there was any over-reaction at all. We were quite impartial. We are put in situations like this and we have a duty to keep the highway clear and allow peaceful picketing.[6]

Despite this violent clash and the arrest of 84 of the 700 demonstrators, relations between the police and the small handful of

APEX pickets themselves remained good. Roy Grantham in particular did his best to co-operate and it was agreed that, next day,
an official picket of six APEX strikers could stand in front of the
police cordon to try to persuade people not to go to work, while
other demonstrators would have to stay behind the cordon or face
charges of obstruction.[7]

Thereafter this pattern continued and, for the next four weeks,
the police held back the demonstrators while the pickets, in front
of the cordon, attempted to persuade the non-union labour force
(now numbering about 270) not to enter the factory. There were
two gates, a front and back entrance, and both were picketed in
this way, though the demonstration was mainly centred on the
front gate.

The violence and the intimidation came entirely from the
demonstrators behind the cordon, and the police successfully pro-
tected both the official pickets and the people going to work from
the violence. No pickets or Grunwick workers were reported as
injured throughout the confrontation. The police and other
injuries all occurred in the battle to maintain this cordon and
permit, as Superintendent Hickman-Smith had said, the peaceful
picketing to continue.

There was, however, considerable danger of molestation by
roving demonstrators of people further out on their way to work.
The workers were easily recognizable, as they walked up the two
long side roads approaching the two gates, because most of them
were Indians and very few other people used these roads, one of
which was a *cul-de-sac* and the other a residential loop road. From
14 June, therefore, the Grunwick management provided buses to
pick them up from their homes and take them back at the end
of the day. Some of the demonstrators followed the buses, took
note of the workers' addresses and photographed them. These
photographs were blown up and exhibited on placards titled
'GRUNWICK SCAB' — but these placards were held up, not by
the pickets in front of the cordon but by demonstrators on the
pavements behind it.[8]

All of these received wide coverage in the press and on television, and aroused much public sympathy for the workers, seen
patiently filing out of the buses and being spoken to by the official
pickets. Behind them the mass of demonstrators screamed abuse
and heaved at the police cordon, which swayed to and fro but did
not break. The official pickets themselves — aware that the

cameras were there — were meticulously correct but, inevitably, shots of them were seldom printed or screened and, to the frustration of Dromey and Grantham, it was the violence of the demonstrators which grabbed the news.

This had a disastrous effect on the progress of the trade union side in the industrial dispute itself. On 16 June, the fourth day of the mass demonstrations, Roy Grantham accepted an invitation from the Grunwick management to speak to a mass meeting of workers inside the factory. He received a hostile reception and the workers voted overwhelmingly not to join the union. Since every one of them had had to run the gauntlet each day to get to work they also, not surprisingly, told him that if any of the sacked strikers were reinstated they would refuse to work with them. NAFF (whose Director, John Gouriet, chaired the meeting) and George Ward ensured that this meeting got wide media coverage. This did much to convince the public that the workers had right on their side, and to discredit the not unreasonable case of the APEX and the 91 strikers, who asked only that both they and those still at work should take part in an impartial ACAS ballot.

INTERVENTION

Meanwhile the postal workers at the Cricklewood sorting office, which handled all the mail for London's NW2 district, decided not to handle any Grunwick mail, and began by blacking 65 bags of mail which were received on 15 June. A legal battle thereafter continued for the next six weeks. Tom Jackson, General Secretary of the UPW, urged the sorters on 28 June to lift the ban and the Post Office warned them that if they did not do so then by 4 July they would be suspended without pay. They refused, and the Cricklewood sorting office closed down altogether. For almost the whole of July, all NW2 pillar boxes were blocked and no one with an NW2 address could have any private or business mail delivered. This, too, was disastrous in terms of public relations. Thanks to the continuing violent demonstration at the factory gates, Grunwick remained front-page news, so the postal workers' action too received massive and adverse publicity. The public reaction against the UPW was predictable. Readers and viewers had no difficulty in identifying with the ordinary people in NW2 — small shopkeepers, families trying to keep in touch, etc. — who were interviewed by reporters seeking the human interest stories which sell newspapers. Editors did not need to have a political motivation to use stories like these. If a public relations consultant had been hired to devise a campaign to encourage 'union-bashing' he could hardly have done better than the leader of the Cricklewood sorters, in harness with the student demonstrators outside the Grunwick gates.

Their opponents, by contrast, displayed a professional touch in handling the media. On 9 July, under the name of 'Operation Pony Express', a team from NAFF picked up all the mail awaiting despatch from the Grunwick factory and distributed it to volunteers for posting individually, all over the country. Postal workers in some sorting offices (e.g. at Luton and Nottingham) spotted the Grunwick brand-names and blacked a few packages but these were soon released. 'Operation Pony Express' captured the attention of the media, and stories of 'citizens outwitting the trade union tyrants' drew jeers for the Cricklewood sorters and the UPW in general, despite Jackson's repeated pleas to the sorters to lift their ban.

The message was, however, getting home. The Post Office quietly allowed a Grunwick representative to collect their 65 mail bags from the NW2 sorting office. The Cricklewood sorters, getting no response to their appeal for sympathy strikes in other sorting offices, called off their boycott and returned to work on 31 July.

Meanwhile, the violent demonstrations at the factory gates approached a peak. By the Friday of the first week, 17 June, there had been 168 arrests and 33 recorded injuries, 28 of them to policemen.[9] The second week saw the intervention of a number of left-wing public figures, ranging from Tribune Group MPs to Arthur Scargill. On Tuesday, 21 June, eight Labour MPs joined the demonstrators – Denis Canavan, Martin Flannery, Joan Maynard, Ian Mikardo, Ronald Thomas, Stanley Thorn, Josephine Richardson and Audrey Wise. All they did was to draw more damaging publicity, this time not only to the unions but also to the Labour Party. One particular story caused some amusement, when Audrey Wise was arrested on a charge of obstructing the police in the execution of their duty. She was alleged to have seized the arm of a policeman who was in the act of arresting a girl demonstrator, upon which the policeman, clearly unaware that she was a Member of Parliament, swung round and bundled her into the van with the words 'Never mind, love, you'll do instead!'[10] This 'bigwig slips on banana skin' story proved irresistible to the press.

Arthur Scargill fared little better. On 23 June he and NUM Vice-President Mick McGahey appeared with 150 Scottish and Yorkshire miners, to 'do a Saltley'.[11] Scargill, on this occasion, made a rare misjudgement of public relations, because the publicity rebounded. By arrangement with the TV camera crews, he performed a march of his 150 miners in a tight military column towards the camera on the approach from their buses to the battlefield. Later, like Audrey Wise, he was arrested. The TV film showed him bursting through the police cordon into the road. At his subsequent trial he pleaded that he had been propelled against his will by pressure from behind and was acquitted but his part in what seemed to be a sordid scuffle contrasted unfavourably with the heroic scale of Saltley and did not enhance his dignity. Furthermore, members of the Yorkshire NUM later accused him of spending £25 000 of their funds on this and his subsequent foray to Grunwick on 11 July. As well as travel costs, this was said to include a payment of £23 to each man − £15 for loss of earnings and £8 subsistence (contrasted with 30p each in the 1974 strike)[12] − and this threw him open to 'rent-a-picket' charges. To a man of his experience, all of these things should have been predictable, and he did no good either for himself or for the strikers.

TELEVISION AND A MILK BOTTLE

Meanwhile the students were doing them no good either. With the end of the university term, more students poured out of Dollis Hill station each morning to greet the arrival of the Grunwick buses. Their numbers reached 1500 on 17 June and 2000 on the day of Scargill's visit, Thursday, 23 June.[13]

This day, in fact, saw the most significant example of the influence the media can have on this kind of demonstration. A demonstrator (who was neither a striker nor an APEX member) threw a milk bottle which struck a policeman, PC Trevor Wilson, on the head and knocked him out. It was then alleged that this or another demonstrator ran up and gouged the unconscious PC Wilson's neck with the broken bottle, and both press and television pictures showed him on the ground with a pool of blood spreading from his head. David Wheeler, writing in the *Listener*, captured the significance of the event.

> 'No genuine trade unionist would have thrown a bottle' said one of the Grunwick strike organizers on ITV, a remark that will have divided the television audience as decisively as the strike itself has divided the nation. The bottle, as all the world knows, struck a young police constable on the head and will now, though shattered, live for years in British political history or (much the same thing) mythology. The incident marked the high point of a bad week for trade unions . . . . However good a case the Grunwick strikers may have against the management, television has ensured that what will stick in people's minds is the blood running from the constable's head as he lay unconscious on the pavement.[14]

If television sometimes encourages or exacerbates violence, on this occasion it undoubtedly acted to restrain it. The Grunwick pickets themselves had no illusions about the damage that the demonstrators were doing to their cause and were genuinely horrified at the bestiality of the attack on PC Wilson. Some of them later visited him in hospital to express their sympathy and their disgust that such a thing should have been done in their name.

Nevertheless, the momentum of the demonstration carried it on into the next day, Friday, 24 June, when 2200 demonstrators were present. The police, too, increased their strength that day to 1521 (compared with 793 on 23 June)[15] and the violence was contained, though there were another 54 arrested and 17 policemen injured. Thereafter, however, the numbers fell − to 900 on the following Monday − and continued to fall, except for isolated demonstrations on 11 July and 8 August described below. Roy Grantham meanwhile agreed with the police − and for the time being carried Jack Dromey with him − to restrict the number of pickets to 500.[16] Dromey dissociated himself from the demonstrators, and twice asked SWP to refrain from handing out what they described as 'strike bulletins'.[17]

The SWP leaders, however, tried their best to keep up the numbers: many of the students had been disgusted by the violence, and in particular by the consequence of it in the PC Wilson incident, which some of them witnessed in person and almost all will have seen on television. SWP propaganda showed signs of hysteria. On 2 July *Socialist Worker* claimed that there was no parliamentary road to socialism and that the police, the judges, the employers' associations and the army were all against them. To defeat them would mean

. . . establishing secret contingents of socialist rank and file police and soldiers, prepared to change sides at crucial moments. It would also mean ensuring that the workers had enough force of their own to protect their rank-and-file soldiers and police against the vengeance of their superiors. There would have to be a workers' militia, prepared to fight the forces of the state until it had a monopoly of armed force in its own hands.[18]

This rather naive call to arms came, in fact, from one of SWP's more highly educated graduates, Chris Harman, who has degrees from both LSE and Leeds University. In the wake of the PC Wilson incident it was hardly likely to appeal either to trade union members or to the majority of demonstrators, whose numbers continued to fall, and it was another example of ineptitude in handling public relations.

There were, nevertheless, two more demonstrations at Grunwick, though the first of these was organized by left-wing trade unionists and not primarily by SWP. Arthur Scargill sent out a call for a 'mass picket' by the trade union movement on Monday, 11 July. The appeal was also taken up by *Socialist Worker* and *Militant* (the paper run by the Trotskyist faction of the Labour Party) and 18 000 turned out. In contrast to those in June this demonstration, like that at Saltley on 10 February, was predominantly made up of trade unionists. There were 3500 police on duty. The crowd initially blocked the factory entrances and, for the first time since the dispute began, the Grunwick workers' bus did not enter the factory on time at 8 a.m. Later in the morning, however, the demonstrators moved off on a peaceful march around the district, led by the unlikely combination of Arthur Scargill and Roy Grantham who was no doubt happy to divert the demonstrators from a bigger and possibly more dangerous confrontation at the gates.

While the march was in progress, the Grunwick bus slipped the workers into the factory. Such violence as there was followed the usual pattern around the gates and there were 70 more arrests, with 30 injuries reported, 18 of them to police. Announcing in Parliament the total arrests and police injuries (377 and 243 respectively) the Home Secretary on 14 July said 'There are people there who are not picketing but are given the name. They are just there to cause trouble.'[19]

Thereafter the temperature and the numbers fell. By Friday, 22 July, the number of 'pickets' had dwindled to 100 — less than the number of workers going to work.[20] Dromey, fearful of a return to apathy and frustration, called for another mass demonstration for 8 August. Roy Grantham, however, said that there were to be no more mass pickets, that no one could be classed as a picket without his authority and that he would not give that authority. To Dromey's discomfiture the Strike Committee supported Grantham and voted against a mass picket. *Socialist Worker*, however, urged its members to defy this decision and 2800 demonstrators turned out, only to be told by the Strike Committee members that they had no right to take over the dispute from people who had been picketing for 50 weeks. There was some shouting but, in response to urgent appeals from Jack Dromey, there was no violence.[21]

That was the end of the intervention of the demonstrators. They had monopolized the media for two weeks and had kept the dispute in the public eye for two months. They had, however, done irreparable damage to the cause, and the morale, of the strikers. The legal battles continued between Ward, APEX and ACAS before the High Court, the Appeal Court and the House of Lords. Lord Scarman carried out an inquiry but, hampered by the requirement to exclude 'any matter before the High Court', was unable to tackle the central issues.

If Ward had ever been willing to compromise, the violence had ruled this out. Further attempts by ACAS to arrange a ballot on the recognition issue led eventually, in January 1978, to a petition to George Ward by 175 out of 176 workers at Grunwick (with only 12 absent) stating 'We the undersigned do not wish to participate in any inquiry or ballot arranged by ACAS. Nor do we wish Grunwick to hand our names and addresses to any party.'[22]

On 12 July, ACAS finally abandoned the dispute and two days later all but two of the 55 remaining strikers voted to abandon the strike and accept APEX offers to help them find other jobs.[23]

THE RISE AND FALL OF A TELEVISION SPECTACULAR

There are many small strikes which are never reported except in the local press. Grunwick might well have been one of these and would in that case probably have ended in some kind of compromise. As it was, under the floodlights of the media, both sides made it an issue of political principle and both sides attempted to exploit the attention of the media to this end.

Attention was first attracted on 5 November 1976 when the strike had been going for a little over two months, over the first attempt to black Grunwick's mail. This brought in NAFF on an issue which provided just the kind of publicity they wanted. The spectacle of a small but successful private employer challenging the power of the mighty unions, and of workers resisting pressure to join a union against their will, would appeal to the kind of recruit they hoped to attract. They claimed at the height of the dispute to be receiving donations of £1000 per day and their membership doubled to 15 000, overtaking that of the National Front. In the long run they gained little, as they incurred heavy legal costs and their aggressive publicity probably drove away a lot of more moderate people who might otherwise have sympathized with their championship of the little man. In 1978 they parted company with John Gouriet and continued their activities with a rather lower profile under a new name — the Freedom Association. Nevertheless, in the case of the Grunwick dispute their publicity campaign was successful in the short term and contributed to the failure of the strike.

After the initial flutter of publicity in November, Mrs Desai and her pickets were largely forgotten in their cold vigil through the winter. It was then that Shirley Williams and her colleagues intervened to get them back into the news — probably with the specific intention of heading off the intervention of the far left which was to prove so damaging to their cause.

This may well also have been the motivation of Roy Grantham in calling for a mass picket in the following month. He certainly lived to regret this decision when it was taken up by *Socialist Worker*. The strike got its publicity, but not of a kind which helped it. The SWP was pursuing, from 1976 to 1979, a policy of demonstrations which led to violent confrontation with the police — at, for example, Hendon, Lewisham, Ladywood, Leicester and Southall, as will be discussed in later chapters.[24]

It was inevitable that the violence at Grunwick would attract the media and especially television. From 13 to 24 June 1977, it was virtually certain that there would be something dramatic to photograph and report. The proximity of Dollis Hill Station guaranteed that there would be a crowd, and there was a high expectation of violence. There was a fixed point, the gate, and a fixed time, 8 a.m., when the workers' buses arrived. Editors could be confident that reporters deployed at that time, with camera teams in well-chosen windows overlooking the gate, were sure of good material — with the rest of the day still free for other assignments in London.

Nevertheless the violence, though achieving its purpose of attracting the cameras, proved wholly counterproductive to its wider aims. Perhaps the most encouraging feature of the whole story was the unquestionable influence of the media in cooling the violence by the dramatic publicity given to its effects — in the picture of PC Wilson in a pool of blood.

4 The Winter of Discontent: Strikes and the Public

FRUSTRATION AND AGGRESSION

Violence is fuelled by frustration and a sense of injustice. A little boy unable to get his hands on the toy he wants will lash out; the more he feels that he has a right to the toy, or that if his brother has one he should have one too, or that its being withheld from him is unfair, the greater the fury of his violence. These are basic human reactions and apply as much to pickets as to anyone else. During the strikes of transport drivers and low paid public service workers in the winter of 1978–9, the strikers felt a sense of injustice that others had something to which they had an equal or greater right, and that their case was not properly understood by the public.

Although there was some very ugly intimidation, physical and psychological, in these strikes, there were far fewer actual injuries than in the cases quoted in previous chapters. This may well have owed something to the publicity given to those injuries by the media (e.g. to PC Wilson at Grunwick) and the consequent public reaction. Nevertheless this enforced restraint may itself have added to the frustration of the pickets and there was a very strong feeling of bitterness amongst trade unionists that the media had a bias against them.

In the introduction and the bibliography there is mention of the number of publications which have sought to prove the general accusation of media bias or to examine the justification for it. Many of these have already been quoted, such as *Bad News* (1976) and *Trade Unions and the Media* (1977). *More Bad News*, although not published until 1980, was also based on earlier industrial disputes, up to 1975. The 1979 strikes were followed by many more publications including Denis MacShane's *Using the Media* (though largely written before 1979) and the TUC pamphlets *A Cause for Concern* and *How to Handle the Media*.

41

Labour Research[1] magazine also launched a vigorous and documented attack on the media in the April 1979 issue.

Faced with these accusations both the IBA and BBC launched comprehensive studies of the television coverage of these strikes. The IBA Audience Research Department carried out a detailed public opinion survey of viewers' perceptions of any bias in the main news coverage of industrial disputes in the early months of 1979[2] which examined public reactions to both the BBC *Nine O'Clock News* and ITN's *News at Ten*. The BBC was asked by its General Advisory Council (GAC) to prepare a report on its 'Coverage of the Industrial Situation January and February 1979' which was debated in October 1979 by the GAC and later published.[3] The following year the subject was again debated in the BBC *Editors* Series.[4] It must, therefore, be one of the best documented and most fully discussed periods in British industrial relations.

A WINTER OF STRIKES

After the alarming rise of unemployment and inflation (peaking at 27 per cent) in the summer of 1975, the Labour Government introduced its Social Contract, an incomes policy which, with TUC cooperation, stemmed the tide and in two years cut inflation back to less than 10 per cent. In 1977, however, the TUC were unable to hold the unions to a third year of voluntary restraint. The government called for a norm of 10 per cent, but the average wage rise was 15 per cent, and inflation began to rise again in 1978. Somewhat desperately the government called for a 5 per cent norm from September 1978. This, however, was too much for the unions to stomach. There was an attempt to hold back the private sector by a Bill to penalize companies which paid more than that rate, but the Bill was thrown out by Parliament, where Mr Callaghan had lost his majority and could only govern with the support of either the Liberals or the Nationalists.

The new wage round began with the Ford Motor Company which settled for 17 per cent. The Labour Government was in a situation in which it could not win. Unless it could hold back wages it knew that its success in pulling back inflation to 8 per cent would be thrown away and the Labour Party would lose the 1979 election; on the other hand, if its attempts to hold back wages led to a winter of industrial strife, this would destroy its claim that only Labour could work with the unions and it would still lose the election. The Labour Government chose the latter and lost with the biggest swing against a government in power since 1945. After the Ford settlement there was really no hope of holding wage rises even to 15 per cent let alone 5 per cent.

The first crises came in January with the lorry drivers' strike. This quickly became bitter because only 40 per cent of drivers were union members. The industry contained many small independent contractors and owner drivers and a lot of big firms operated their own transport. The highly flexible nature of most transport made secondary picketing the only feasible way of interrupting it, and the TGWU strategy was to block the ports and the sources of key raw materials. The result was an estimated loss of £1500 million in export orders and 235 000 other workers laid off. The strike was therefore very unpopular. There was also some ugly intimidation on the picket lines, because individual lorry drivers are very vulnerable, while their lorries can be lethal. One picket was run over and killed in Aberdeen and it is something of a miracle that he was the only one.

Just as the drivers settled (for 21 per cent) a widespread strike of low paid public service workers began, ranging from hospital staff to road gritters. That both of these caused loss of life is beyond doubt — the latter because February 1979 was one of the coldest on record. Again the strike was unpopular, though there was more public sympathy for the plight of a school cleaner with a family whose wage was so low that he had no savings to fall back on to withstand a strike, than for lorry drivers claiming starvation on three or four times the income of an old age pensioner. Nevertheless both strikes caused a great deal of suffering to members of the public, who read, watched and listened anxiously to the reports and forecasts on the media.

COVERAGE BY THE MEDIA

The media generally tried to answer the immediate questions people wanted to ask: are the antagonists digging their heels in, or are they moving towards a settlement — in other words, are the shops going to run out of food and will our school remain closed? The tabloids competed with headlines calculated to capitalize on anxiety, anger and alarm. NEW STRIKE COULD HALT BRITAIN (*Mail*), LORRY STRIKE THREAT TO FOOD (*Express*), BRITAIN UNDER SIEGE (*Mail*), PANIC IN THE SHOPS (*Express*), FAMINE THREAT — FOOD STORES EMPTY IN TEN DAYS (*Sun*) referred to the lorry drivers' strike. The public service strikes were greeted with CHAOS ON ALL SIDES (*Sun*), FOUR MILLION CHILDREN ARE BLOCKADED FROM SCHOOL (*Sun*), IT'S NO MERCY UNTIL FURTHER NOTICE (*Mail*), LIVES AT RISK AS STRIKERS SHOW NO MERCY (*Yorkshire Post*), LIFE OR DEATH PICKET (*Express*), HOSPITAL WORKERS TIGHTEN NOOSE (*Lancashire Evening Post*), CANCER WARD TORMENT (*Express*), WHAT RIGHT HAVE THEY GOT TO PLAY GOD WITH MY LIFE? (from a heart surgery patient) (*Express*), TARGET FOR TODAY – SICK CHILDREN (*Mail*), DEADLINE MIDNIGHT – POLICE AND TROOPS GO ON STANDBY FOR SOS CALLS (*Sun*) and YOU NAME IT – THEY'LL STOP IT (*Mail*).[5]

A Gallup Poll published in the *Daily Telegraph* on 1 February was said by the newspaper to mark the lowest public rating for trade unions ever measured by Gallup in 40 years of polling, 84 per cent expressing the view that the unions had too much power. Other polls have confirmed — and continued to confirm in 1980 — that the majority of trade union members took this view. The TUC, in *Cause for Concern*, blamed the media coverage for this. The momentum of this unpopularity brought in a Conservative Government in May 1979 with a mandate to curb the power of unions and pickets.

Public figures also made some wild predictions of the effects of the transport strike. ICI forecast that they would shut down all plants within a week, but the strike continued and all plants remained open. Chancellor Denis Healey forecast 'a million laid off by the end of next week'. Others said 'two million'. The maximum, in the event, was 235 000.[6]

The TUC (*Cause for Concern*), Denis MacShane (*Using the Media*), Paul Walton (in BBC's *The Editors*, 16 June 1980) and *Labour Research*, April 1979, all complained that the media were overwhelmingly biased against the trade unions. The headlines selected above by *Labour Research* suggest that this certainly applied to the press. There is some evidence that it also applied to television current affairs programmes, but not to the main television news bulletins — according to the IBA survey of viewers' perceptions. Taking both the transport and public service disputes, 12 per cent of the audience of ITN's *News at Ten* thought the coverage was biased in favour of management and 13 per cent biased in favour of workers. For the BBC *Nine O'Clock News* the figures were 12 per cent and 9 per cent respectively. In both cases, the great majority found no appreciable bias either way (ITN: 75 per cent; BBC: 79 per cent).[7] Quoting from *More Bad News* Paul Walton complained that in the 1975 disputes managers got more time on the air than trade union officials or strikers, but the BBC study found that in the 'Winter of Discontent' the reverse was true – that management was too sparsely represented, that 'trade unionists were by far the most widely represented group on the air' and that 'the employers (Government Ministers excluded) barely advanced beyond the role of faceless men'.[8]

On the other hand, the IBA survey found that most viewers thought the treatment of employers' spokesmen interviewed on ITN and BBC News was more sympathetic than the treatment of strikers, with treatment of trade union officials being roughly neutral – neither harsh nor sympathetic. There was, not surprisingly, a difference in balance between the perception of Labour, Liberal and Conservative viewers. Liberal viewers did not reflect the general consensus about the treatment of strikers, the majority of those questioned believing that strikers had been interviewed too sympathetically. The great majority of Labour voters, however, felt that the interviewing of strikers had been too harsh.[9]

This suggests that the television viewers' reports tended to reinforce views already held. Liberally minded viewers were shocked by the intimidation of individual lorry drivers by large groups of pickets – compared by some newspapers to the Nazi bully-boys who shouted abuse on the streets of Munich and Berlin in the 1930s; these viewers would no doubt have liked to say a thing or two to those pickets and felt that the interviewers were letting them off too lightly. By contrast, trade unionists who had themselves been on picket lines felt that the television cameras recorded only the few moments when violence threatened or when intimidation was evident, ignoring the hours during which the pickets had been standing, icy cold and bored stiff, with only an occasional driver to persuade. Peaceful persuasion is not news but when, after all this, some cowboy tried to drive on and break the picket line, the pickets would react and the microphone thrust into their faces might pick up some fairly forthright comments. It was those short dramatic snatches which found a slot in the fierce competition for the few minutes available for the report in the main evening news bulletin. Editors know well enough that if ITN is boring, viewers will switch to the BBC, and vice versa. The inevitable result was that the presentation of just the highlights of intimidation in-flamed both those who sympathized with the pickets and those who did not.

THE BACKGROUND TO THE DISPUTES

One of the most widely voiced criticisms of the media was that they failed to give a fair background to the disputes. Critics[10] con-sidered that more depth was needed on both sides; to make a fair judgement of the lorry drivers' strike the viewers needed to know more about, on the one hand, the structure of the transport industry, the union's difficulty in preventing the strike being out-flanked and the family life, hardships and responsibilities of a heavy goods driver; on the other hand, they needed to know the financial realities of running a haulage business and whether paying the wages demanded was really likely to cause bankruptcies and unemployment. The reader or viewer should have been given the kind of information needed to judge how far the two sides were to blame for the dispute and how far they were justified in holding out.

It is also the duty of the media to disclose the real effect of a dispute on the public, so that both sides not only know what these effects will be but also know that the public know. Every shop steward knows that, to keep a man on strike, he must insulate him from the direct effect that his action will have on the people who depend upon his work. No ambulance driver, faced with an injured child, would refuse to take it to hospital. No bus driver would deliberately leave a load of grannies and mothers and children standing marooned in the rain if he could see them, as actual people, face to face. A striker whose action is causing others to be laid off or lose their jobs would at least think again if he actually met some of the men and their families and saw what he was doing to them. Seeing them on television is the next best thing. Compassion is the foundation of freedom and most people are compassionate. It is both fair and healthy to allow that compassion to operate by disclosure of these effects, though there is an important line between honest disclosure and calculated exag-geration designed to arouse passions rather than compassion.

Here again there is no substitute for journalistic integrity. This question will arise again in Chapter 8.

The public, as well as the employers and union officials and strikers, also have a right to reliable estimates of the long-term effects of a dispute on the community — e.g. on the balance of payments, loss of future orders and loss of jobs. The critics of the coverage of the 1979 disputes also suggested that it would be desirable to look back from time to time, over the subsequent year, to analyse how the estimates of long-term damage had in practice worked out.

The problem is that the number of newspaper readers who read such background pieces and the number of viewers who watch programmes about it when they are offered are very few. Only one person reads one of the quality papers (*Telegraph, Guardian, The Times, Financial Times*) for every eight who read the popular press. Over 20 million people watch one or more TV news bulletins every day. Current affairs programmes (e.g. *Panorama* or *Weekend World*) have far smaller audiences and special interest programmes and documentaries, such as *The Money Programme* and *The Risk Business* smaller still. The balance between the roles of entertaining and informing is tilted towards entertaining simply because if a programme fails to entertain (which includes exciting interest) the viewer will switch off and not be informed either. An earlier IBA survey[11] found that of news and current affairs programmes audience interest in industrial disputes and strikes, the Social Contract, Trade Union conferences and the stock market was rated low, far lower, for example, than national disasters (floods, etc.), North Sea oil, the housing problem or the Royal Family (the top four).

An associated problem is that the time devoted to an item on the *Nine O'Clock News* or *News at Ten* is seldom more than four minutes, often two minutes or less. Items on a popular magazine programme like *Nationwide* usually last about five minutes. Only on documentary and current affairs programmes like *Panorama, Newsweek, Newsnight, The Money Programme* or *The Risk Business* will any one topic be examined for 30 minutes or more, so the mass audience on television, like the readers of the popular press, go short on background.[12] This is hard to overcome but not impossible to alleviate. Even a few words of explanation can make the difference between an item which is misleading or inflammatory and an item which is balanced, fair and reasonable. The

bare news report, as has been shown, tends to reinforce prejudices
on both sides.

THE BALANCE SHEET

Do the media, on balance, exacerbate industrial disputes and
increase violence on picket lines? On the evidence available,
especially from the three cases of Saltley, Grunwick and the
'Winter of Discontent' they would seem, paradoxically, to exacerbate the disputes but to decrease the violence.

The media can never be completely fair but, while every newspaper has a declared political stance well recognized by its readers,
the radio and television news media are statutorily required to be
unbiased and, although *Bad News* and *More Bad News* put the
case to the contrary, they generally are unbiased and are considered by most of the public to be unbiased. Most people get their
news from radio or television. Since it is the sense of injustice
rather than injustice itself which inflames a man to violence, the
fact that no one has been killed on a picket line, barring accidents,
since 1911, i.e. before either radio or television began to broadcast, speaks for itself.

The chief problem, however, is not one of bias but of time and
space. A two-minute TV news item can show only the highlights of
a day's picketing and these give neither a true nor a fair picture.
Like the quality papers, the current affairs and documentary programmes which do have time to give the background are seen only
by a small minority — consisting mainly of people least likely to be
personally involved in a confrontation on a picket line, but who are
likely to be adversely affected by a strike. It is, however, in the
interest of everyone, strikers included, to understand the background, including the cost of the dispute to the strikers themselves
(e.g. if it will take three years to make up the lost pay) and to the
community, both in the short term and the long term. The problem of background needs urgent study by the media.

The media can no more be 100 per cent fair than the public can
be 100 per cent fair — or logical. People will press for pay rises
themselves, but resent it when others do so. A free and competitive
press inevitably reflects majority opinion, but this is far preferable
to a press controlled by a monopoly (capitalist or union closed
shop), or, worst of all, by a government.

If the public is sympathetic, the press will reflect this sympathy, as with the miners before 1971, the firemen before 1977, the ambulancemen before 1979. When an essential public service is hit by strikes, the only sufferers are the public so the strikers forfeit the sympathy of the public and therefore also of the media.

The media can, however, precipitate conflict and violence by being consciously or unconsciously inflammatory – e.g. the reports of the 'Mountain of Coke' at Saltley in 1972; or by speculation to feed the public anxiety about shortages which may lead to alarm – as was proved in January 1979.

The media can be 'used' by ministers, employers, unions, politically-motivated journalists or political activists of both sides. The exaggerated predictions of doom in January 1979 must surely have had the aim of deterring the strikers though, being false, they deservedly rebounded. Shirley Williams and her colleagues tried to use the media to overcome the frustration of the forlorn Grunwick pickets. This too rebounded, rather unkindly, by being linked with the violence of the demonstrators a few weeks later, which it was probably intended to forestall. And when that violence began, both the far right (NAFF) and the far left (SWP) tried to use the media to their own advantage. NAFF succeeded but SWP's attempt rebounded, contributing to the failure of the strike itself, for which SWP have not been forgiven.

The media can exacerbate violence, or cause conflict to flare up, when people are encouraged by the presence of the camera to act up – another way of trying to use the media to attract attention. The camera can also exacerbate violence by putting pickets on their mettle. Because the whole world was watching, the miners at Saltley felt they *had* to win or the other pickets all over the country might lose heart. The result was the most violent picket since 1911.[13]

On the other hand, the media can also restrain violence or at least keep it within bounds, because all sides know how adverse is the British public's reaction to it. When the pushing and shoving at Saltley threatened to escalate into something more vicious, Arthur Scargill thereafter did his best to restrain it. He did the same at Hadfields during the 1980 steel strike where the mere presence of the mass picket, with its shouted abuse and threats, was enough to intimidate the private sector steelworkers into staying away from work next day. He knew that if the pickets actually got amongst the men going to work there would be fighting and men injured in front of the television cameras and that this would do no good either to his own image or to the steelworkers, so he co-operated with the police in placing the mass picket safely behind a double cordon. Scargill had also been present at Grunwick on 23 June 1977 and he knew the strength of the public reaction to the television pictures of PC Wilson bleeding on the pavement.

The biggest problem of all, however, is that bare news reporting tends to reinforce prejudices and harden the attitudes of both sides in a dispute, even if it does not increase the violence. Since pickets are seldom seen on television unless they are being either violent or intimidatory, they may unjustly be saddled with a bully-boy image. This applies especially to the short news items on the news – the programmes the pickets will watch when they are off duty. This causes them to feel unfairly treated and arouses their anger.

Journalists have a heavy responsibility if they wittingly fuel this anger. A few will actually wish to do so, some for political reasons and others to make exciting news. Most, however, do not wish to exacerbate the conflict at all. To avoid doing so, they must not only be honest and fair, but must also seek the elusive element of background. Violence and the demand for an oppressive reaction to violence will be less likely if each side at least understands that the other side does have a case to answer; also if everyone concerned has a better idea of the real costs and consequences of the dispute not only to themselves but to the consumers, and, in the longer term, to the economy and to the future prospects of employment and earnings.

This leads to the longer-term effect of industrial disputes on the prospects of preserving a liberal and non-violent society. If the prognosis in the Introduction is correct, the greatest threats of violence in British society will arise from racial conflict and high unemployment and these, as will emerge in subsequent chapters, are closely linked. The reaction to such violence is the likeliest cause of intolerance and the curtailment of press and personal freedoms. Journalists and others who knowingly or recklessly exacerbate damaging industrial conflicts may therefore be contributing, in the long run, not only to a less prosperous and more violent society, but also to erosion of the very civil liberties they cherish.

Part II

Demonstrations and the Institutions of Law and Order

5 Political Demonstrations

PERFORMING FOR THE CAMERA

The right of assembly to draw attention to a grievance, to demonstrate support for a political view or to apply pressure for change is as fundamental as the right to free elections, free speech and freedom of the press. It is normally only the small political parties, the extremes of right and left, who need to demonstrate to make their voices heard. Neither has any more right or any less right to demonstrate than the other. Neither has any right to prevent the other from demonstrating and, so long as these freedoms are maintained, no one has any right to use violence in demonstrations.

The Metropolitan Police recorded 1321 political demonstrations in London in 1972—4 of which only 54 involved disorder. In these 54, however, 623 arrests were made and 373 people injured, 297 of them being police officers.[1] The 54 included the demonstration in Red Lion Square in which a man was killed — the first in a demonstration in Britain for 55 years.

By 1977 political demonstrations had become more violent. Within a few summer weeks of that year 243 policemen were injured at Grunwick alone and these with another 114 at Lewisham and Ladywood brought the total number of policemen injured in those three demonstrations to 357. This was more than in all the London demonstrations in 1972—4 put together. All of these three incidents involved the Socialist Workers' Party (SWP). 1978 was a quieter year but in 1979 another man was killed in a riot at Southall, in which 97 policemen and 64 members of the public were injured and in which the SWP again played a major part.

The very meaning of the word 'demonstration' indicates that its essential and legitimate purpose is to attract attention. In today's world this means attracting the attention of the mass media. In a local protest about, say, the lack of a pedestrian crossing, the

53

organizers will try to make sure that at least the local press report it and, if possible, the national press. A big demonstration in London about, say, the treatment of Jews in the Soviet Union, will be deemed to have achieved little unless it gets at least a mention in the main TV news bulletins.

Sometimes the mere size of a demonstration is enough to attract such attention. If 100 000 trade unionists assemble in Hyde Park to protest peacefully against government policy that in itself is news; and this is one of the classic and legitimate functions of the right of assembly: to demonstrate the breadth of support and solidarity.

More often, sadly, the national news media will not bother to send their reporters to cover a demonstration unless there is a prospect of either significant disruption (e.g. the blocking of a motorway) or violence. Of the two, violence is the more attractive. There is thus an almost irresistible temptation for the organizers of a national political demonstration to arouse the expectation of some kind of confrontation – and confrontation needs an adversary.

One possible adversary is a rival demonstration. When the National Front (NF) plan a march in a certain city, their preparations are such that the Anti-Nazi League (ANL) and the SWP are bound to know about it in advance. Similarly an NF march is a godsend to the SWP. Both are sure of publicity and for this they feed upon each other.

The other choice for an adversary is the police. The aim must be to ensure that the media anticipate an immovable object facing an irresistible force. A march directed at a place which the police are bound to protect – such as the American Embassy in Grosvenor Square – is one answer. The other is to threaten to close with a rival demonstration in circumstances likely to occasion a breach of the peace which the police are again bound by the law to prevent.

The expectation of dramatic events having been aroused, the reporters and cameramen will be there. If, however, everything is peaceful, there is a powerful temptation, especially for a young journalist trying to make his name, to encourage the participants to give him something to report.

The mere prospect of a major confrontation is in itself news-worthy. People will anxiously pick newspapers off the news stands if they have headlines predicting a violent confrontation next day or next week. The editor, having predicted it, will cover it.

His reporters will make the best of the event that they can. The demonstrators may act up to the cameras so the prediction may be self-fulfilling.

A valuable study of this phenomenon was made by the Leicester University Centre for Mass Communications Research under Professor J. D. Halloran.[2] They did a content analysis of both the pre-event and after-event coverage of the march on Grosvenor Square in October 1968. The declared purpose of the demonstration was to demand the end of US intervention in Vietnam. There had been a similar demonstration in March 1968, in which 117 people had been injured. There had been some particularly dramatic press and television coverage[3] of the confrontation outside the US Embassy showing, for example, a policeman being held by one demonstrator and kicked in the face by another. Television viewers saw policemen being bombarded with injurious missiles and (perhaps even more emotive for British viewers) police horses whinnying in terror as they slid on ball-bearings strewn under their feet. Public passions ran high.

The March demonstration in Grosvenor Square was followed in the next few weeks by the far more violent clashes in the student revolt in Paris in May and June and the fighting between demonstrators and police at the Democratic Convention in Chicago. The theme was always the same – long-haired students fighting helmeted policemen. There was also a strong international element with, for example, American and German students both in Paris and London. The leading figure in the Grosvenor Square demonstration in London had been a Pakistani immigrant, Tariq Ali.

Halloran records that, as the day for the October march on Grosvenor Square approached, the media built up a public apprehension amounting almost to hysteria, based on a number of phobias, notably students, foreign leadership and violence. In the event Tariq Ali, perhaps himself alarmed by the hysteria and by the adverse public reaction to the March demonstration, agreed with the police to lead the marchers (estimates of their number vary from 30 000 to 50 000) away from Grosvenor Square and to go instead to Hyde Park.[4] About 4000 defied Tariq Ali's lead and went into Grosvenor Square, where there was a confrontation with the police, who were there in force.[5] A few hundred demonstrators made mass charges at the police cordon but the police absorbed these charges with skilful sponge tactics and no one was seriously injured. The confrontation was relatively good humoured and few journalists would have predicted the way the day ended, when the police and demonstrators linked arms and sang 'Auld Lang Syne'.

This was, of course, reported by most of the media but Halloran argues that they concentrated much more on reporting what they had predicted; and that they focused on whatever foreigners they could find, on making the pushing and shoving seem as violent as possible and, in particular, on the arrests of students.[6]

Before 1968 it had not been easy for the media to find much violence to report on the streets of Britain, nor was there much in the years that followed. No one had been killed in a riot since 1919, when two looters had been shot by the army during a police strike in Liverpool. That record, however, was shattered in 1974 when Kevin Gately was killed in a riot in Red Lion Square, the first of what was to become a series of clashes arising from left-wing demonstrations attempting to block or break up NF marches. The police on this occasion succeeded in keeping the NF and the counter-demonstrators apart and Gately was in the middle of a crowd which had charged and been checked by a police cordon. He fell and was trampled on by the crowd. As in Grosvenor Square, the assault on the police was led by the International Marxist Group (IMG). There was a judicial inquiry into Kevin Gately's death by Lord Scarman who found that he was in the middle of the crowd when he fell and that 'a heavy responsibility rests on those who instigated and led that assault'.[7]

The IMG received very adverse publicity, both in the immediate reports of the riot in the media and in the comment arising from the Scarman Inquiry. Perhaps for this reason, they thereafter used the technique of mass demonstrations much less frequently, and particularly tried to avoid violent confrontations with the police. The opposition to the subsequent NF marches (especially in 1977 and 1979) was led by the SWP.

A few weeks after the riot in Red Lion Square, there was another violent incident which produced valuable lessons for the media and for the police. As a final fling for the hippy counter-culture of the late 1960s there was a series of Free Festivals in Windsor Great Park, advertised as 'social and political protest, drugs and mass sexual activities'. The third of this series was in August 1974, attended by 8000, mainly students. After five days 364 had been arrested, 296 of them for drug offences. The camp was becoming a health hazard and there had been a number of violent confrontations in the streets of Windsor between campers and residents. Since camping in the Park was in itself a breach of the law, the police broadcast instructions on the sixth day to clear the site. Most of the campers left but when the police moved in at 11 a.m. on Thursday 29 August about 500 remained, armed with sticks and bottles and other missiles and prepared for a siege. The organizers directed the resistance through the public address system. They also selected one of the pop group stages for a 'last stand' and it was here that they displayed notable skill in using the media.

They positioned two buses beside this stage and invited the BBC to position their camera on one and ITV on the other, telling them that this was where the main confrontation was going to be. In the fighting that ensued 70 policemen and 46 of the campers were injured. Feelings were running high because a class element came into the confrontation. The predominantly working-class policemen were disgusted by both the physical filth and the abuse of the predominantly middle-class hippies. There were some dramatic and violent pictures and a number of policemen drew their truncheons. Public sympathy was strongly on the side of the police and the incident eventually rebounded in that the attempt to hold a fourth Free Festival in 1975 at Watchfield drew very few people and the idea petered out. Nevertheless the police at Windsor Park did not show up at their best and the 'media ambush' certainly succeeded. It was perhaps with this in mind that the International Socialists organized another kind of media ambush at West Hendon in 1976.

THE EXPLOITATION OF UNEMPLOYMENT AND INDUSTRIAL CONFLICT

The International Socialists (IS) — now renamed SWP — were a university-based movement which has since 1973 had between 3000 and 5000 members. Most of their leaders have been graduates, and middle-class students have predominated amongst their membership. They began as a rather theoretical study group, dedicated to the Trotskyist ideal of world revolution. After 1973, however, they responded to the desire of radical university students to shed their middle-class background. They worked hard not only to cultivate a working-class image (their change of title at the end of 1976 was a symptom of this) but also to involve themselves in industrial conflict in order to attract more manual workers as members. At first they tried to do this by encouraging IS graduates to take up manual work in factories and to volunteer for duty as shop stewards. By doing intensive study of regulations and using their brains and articulacy in negotiations with employers, they hoped to earn support by gaining benefits for their fellow workers on the shopfloor. They sometimes made a considerable impact on their industries, one graduate from Exeter University, for example, claiming to have reduced the production of British Leyland by £30 million since he joined them. Nevertheless, most of them were soon detected as middle-class radicals interested more in revolution and disruption than in their declared aim of bringing better wages and working conditions. IS therefore turned more of their attention to the white-collar unions, notably the journalists' (NUJ), teachers' (NUT) and civil service unions. They formed 'Rank and File' movements designed to discredit moderate union leaders and supplant other militants (especially the CPGB).

Though they were (and remain) more successful in white-collar than in manual workers' unions, their best chance came outside the unions altogether — amongst the unemployed. In the wake of the inflation of 1975, unemployment reached nearly 1½ million in January 1976. There was much disaffection both with the Labour Government and with the moderate union leadership with which it was closely associated. At the end of February 1976, just before Harold Wilson handed over as Prime Minister to James Callaghan, IS organized a 'Right to Work March' from Manchester to London, to take three weeks and to end with a mass rally in the Albert Hall on 20 March.

It aimed to recall the Jarrow March of 1936 but was a very small affair. IS mobilized 90 marchers and, though 12 of those eventually charged with assault on the police were students or graduates, most of the 90 were *bona fide* unemployed manual workers. IS aimed to raise about £200 to finance each marcher and, since they claimed that they received much free hospitality en route, there were inevitably 'rent-a-mob' accusations.[8]

The aim, clearly, was to attract publicity and to mobilize anti-government feeling all the way down the route. Had there been confrontation with the police at various points they would no doubt have got the publicity they wanted, but the police took great trouble to avoid clashes. As a result, they approached the outskirts of London having been virtually ignored by the media so, unless the rally at the Albert Hall was to be a flop, drastic action was needed.

On 19 March 1976 they entered the Metropolitan Police area. Escorted by eight police officers, they marched down the busy A41 trunk road into West Hendon and approached the crossing over the North Circular Road at Staples' Corner. Here, a flyover was under construction but the bridge over the North Circular was still incomplete. Ignoring police direction to use the slip road, they marched up the ramp to the bridge to talk to the construction workers, most of whom were on piecework and resented the interruption. They then had to march back down the ramp and do a U-turn into the slip road at the bottom. The Chief Inspector in charge of their escort, seeing that the traffic lights further back had just released a flow of vehicles, raised his arms to check the marchers until the road was clear.

This was the moment chosen to spring the ambush. The leading marchers suddenly set upon the Chief Inspector and his Sergeant, knocked them to the ground and 'put the boot in'. Both were severely injured, the Chief Inspector being kicked in the crotch and the Sergeant requiring 14 stitches in the head. The remaining six policemen in the escort ran forward to help them and they too were beaten up. The small West Hendon Police Station was only 200 yards away on the slip road and other policemen, hearing the noise, ran out of the station to join in. They were still hopelessly outnumbered, however, and when they attempted to make arrests they too were attacked and a general riot ensued. Forty-one policemen were injured, three of them seriously.

As at Windsor Park the site was well chosen. Positioned on the ramp overlooking the slip road was the Editor of *Socialist Worker*, Paul Foot, with four cameramen. The *Socialist Worker* printing presses were standing by for an all-night run to produce a special edition for issue next morning to publicize the Albert Hall rally. The photographs selected were those which showed policemen in the fight with raised fists or attempting forcibly to arrest one of the marchers. There were none, obviously, showing policemen being kicked on the ground or severely injured (as one was) by a block of concrete dropped on his head from the ramp above. Though none of the marchers was seriously hurt, the impression given by the pictures was that of policemen attacking the marchers. Apart from Paul Foot and these four photographers, there were no other reporters or cameramen present and, whether this was by accident or design, it had the effect of ensuring that the only photographs which reached the national press were those selected by this same group.

In the long term, as so often, the propaganda effect of the violence rebounded and it proved counter-productive. After another incident a few weeks later Len Murray, the TUC General Secretary, dismissed the 'Right to Work' demonstrators as 'Trotskyist political bootboys responsible to no-one but themselves'.[9] Nevertheless the 'graduate godfathers' who led the IS were satisfied to have presented the police on the media in a violent role and felt sufficiently encouraged by their own appearance on the media in the role of champions of the unemployed to rename themselves the Socialist Workers' Party.

It was under this title that they took up the cause of the Grunwick strikers in 1977, as described in Chapter 3, in which they hoped again both to identify with people out of work (in this case the strikers who had been sacked) and to confront the police, whom they aimed to cast in the role of protecting the system and the organizations which had caused the unemployment.

Grunwick also brought in the growingly attractive element of racial conflict, though this was blurred by the fact that not only the strikers but also the employer and the employees still going to work were almost all coloured immigrants. Nevertheless, the fact that unemployment amongst coloured immigrants was generally higher than among whites, and that there was more than average friction between coloured people and police, presented SWP with the opportunity to combine the exploitation of industrial conflict and unemployment as a focus for demonstrations with the exploitation of racial strife.

THE EXPLOITATION OF RACIAL CONFLICT

A multiracial society offers a wonderfully explosive mixture for those who wish to ignite it. The combustibility of the mixture is perhaps best illustrated by two scenarios described to the author by a police sergeant in Lewisham.[10]

Scenario I. A shoe shop. Enter a tall black teenager with a Rastafarian[11] haircut. He asks for a pair of shoes. The small white girl assistant fits them on. He then picks up his old shoes and begins to walk out without paying. She remonstrates, he shouts, and the manageress joins in. He warns the two ladies that, if they report the incident, he will break up the shop and that if he is arrested his friends will not only break up the shop but carve up the ladies too. He strides out leaving them trembling with fright. They report nothing to the police, but they never miss a chance of retelling the story, with growing indignation, to their friends.

Scenario II. Bus stop. A pair of patrolling policemen see a pair of black youths in the queue whose demeanour somehow suggests that they are not there to catch the bus. The policemen watch discreetly. There is a movement. They stride forward, plunge a hand into one of the boys' pockets and pull out a purse. 'Excuse me, madam, is this yours?' 'My goodness, it certainly is!' The two black boys are led away. The black community (and *Flame*, the SWP paper for black readers) fume. 'If those had been white boys the police would not have bothered to watch them. They just lean on the blacks – and then claim that blacks commit most of the crimes.'

So the flames are fanned on both sides. In this atmosphere, it is no surprise that the National Front (along with its splinter-group the National Party) collected 44 per cent of the vote in a 1976 local election in Lewisham – the highest proportion they have ever polled.

The National Front attracts mainly two kinds of recruit. One is, typically, a middle-aged shopkeeper, losing his business to an Asian extended family which has opened an all-night store. The Asians, perhaps a gifted and educated family dispossessed and driven out of Uganda by Idi Amin, are willing to work a 14-hour day, seven days a week, to create a new life for themselves. Being one family, they have no trouble over wages, or unions, or working hours or even, provided that they sell only authorized items of food, with by-laws. The white shopkeeper cannot hope to compete with their prices even with normal hours, and certainly not if his staff works overtime. He has other things to do than work a 14-hour day seven days a week himself but, unless he does, the Asians will bankrupt him. 'I fought in the war to save Britain for the British, not for immigrants. Send the bastards home before they take over our country', he says.

The other typical NF member is younger and comes from a deprived home. He probably has no qualifications, no job and no prospect of a job. His family is sick of having him hanging around at home. His life offers him nothing — apart from his friends with whom he has shared a bleak childhood, rebellious schooldays and a defiance of what the world calls failure. They probably also share a bitter pride as a group, and a more positive pride as supporters of their football team. They nevertheless resent being at the bottom of the heap and look for someone to kick. The blacks — especially those with their own group pride as 'Rastas' — kick back. The white boys, for security, seek a larger group. They find the National Front, which wants to send the blacks home and also calls on a bigger and more respectable pride — in the Union Jack and in the past and potential greatness of Great Britain.

As with any conflict worthy of the name, all sides have a case. The Asian shopkeeper and his family have a right to create a new life and to enjoy the fruits of hard work. The white shopkeeper has a right to a livelihood without the choice between a 14-hour day and bankruptcy. The black teenager, whose parents, not he himself, chose that he should live in Britain, has as much right to a job as the white teenager. The white teenager has the right to criticize a political leadership which, in a country with high unemployment, added 2 million blacks to the population. None of them, however, have any justification for using violence, however justified their frustration. Those who exploit that frustration to ignite violence, to seek publicity for political ends, have far more to answer for, while those few reporters or cameramen who knowingly or recklessly exploit it just to create news are contemptible.

In organizing a march in Lewisham on 13 August 1977 the NF, bearing in mind the explosive situation described above, were calculatedly playing with fire. So were those who called for counter-demonstrations. Both knew well enough that if the NF march passed peacefully through the streets unopposed it would achieve nothing and bring the NF no publicity. The SWP leaders were politically educated and experienced and must have realized that violent opposition to the march would bring publicity to the NF and also exacerbate the racial conflict in Lewisham. Since the NF try assiduously to present a law-abiding image of co-operating precisely with police directions, the SWP were not so stupid as to imagine that the publicity would harm the NF more than it harmed the SWP, whose members certainly would (and did) use violence both against the NF and the police. It is therefore only possible to deduce that the true aim was to discredit the police, first, by casting them in the role of protectors of the racist NF and secondly by obtaining reports and pictures of policemen using force to arrest 'legitimate, liberally minded and, in many cases, coloured protestors'.

The concerted nature and the political purpose behind this attack on the reputation of the police is examined more fully in the next chapter. The techniques at Lewisham were, first, to arouse the interest of the media (as described for the Grosvenor Square demonstration) in the prospect of a confrontation so that the reporters and cameras would be there; and then, to have so inflamed the coloured teenagers in Lewisham that they would seize the opportunity of attacking the police. An examination of the issues of *Flame* and *Socialist Worker* on the day of the demonstration and before it, leaves no doubt about that,[12] and their subsequent justification of the violence was equally significant.[13] The worst violence, in fact, occurred after the NF marchers had finished their meeting and left the district in a special train, when the now thoroughly aroused black teenagers launched a series of attacks on the Lewisham Police Station and on police vehicles in its vicinity. This was when most of the 56 injuries to policemen were inflicted.

The SWP had aroused the violence and they had also aroused the interest of the media. The media thereupon both predicted the violence and reported it, and all concerned achieved their publicity. In the case of the NF this helped both their recruiting and their subsequent electoral voting strength. In the case of the SWP, as usual, it rebounded after a temporary boost to recruiting of students and blacks. Their primary aim, however, was achieved. The public image of the police as an unarmed and non-violent force was subtly eroded, not only by pictures of violence but still more by pictures of policemen for the first time in England deployed with perspex riot shields.

Two days later after a similar publicity build-up, the SWP gathered to break up a NF election meeting at the Ladywood by-election in Birmingham. The cameras were there in force and again the police used perspex shields. On this occasion the police held the NF and SWP completely apart, so the SWP attack was solely directed at the police, of whom 58 (one in seven of those on duty) were injured, six of them seriously. Again the NF gained, doubling its share of the poll in the by-election (5.7 per cent), beating the Liberals into fourth place, while the SWP candidate got only 1 per cent of the vote.[14] Since no less than 40 per cent of the Ladywood voters were coloured, and the SWP presented themselves as their champions against the NF, they themselves had clearly gained nothing directly from the publicity. Once again, bearing in mind their political sophistication, it must be assumed that they knew that this would be so and that their target was again to present the police in a violent situation on the television screens.

The public reaction against both the NF and the SWP, however, was such that there were no further incidents of this kind until the run up to the general election in 1979. The main confrontations were at Leicester and Southall on 21 and 23 April. Since the main issues in the election were taking most of the attention of the media, these demonstrations received much less prior coverage than usual. At Leicester the police handled a large NF march and ANL counter-demonstration with great skill, deploying 4500 policemen to keep the two apart. There were few injuries and few arrests and therefore little publicity.

The same would have applied to Southall except for the death of Blair Peach, one of the ANL demonstrators. In the demonstration as a whole 97 policemen were injured. In one confrontation on a road junction a policeman was hit by a brick which fractured his jaw. A Special Patrol Group Unit was ordered to disperse the relatively small crowd at a street corner from which the brick had been thrown. While the police were pursuing them down a side-street, Blair Peach was struck on the head and later died. The verdict of the jury at the Coroner's inquest was 'death by mis-adventure'. This was taken to imply that he died as a result of a blow by a policeman in execution of his duty but that the police-man was not using excessive force. The finding was unsatisfactory in that the man who struck the blow was never identified and none of the policemen who took part in the clearing of the street admitted striking Blair Peach. The incident provided a powerful weapon for the ANL and for others who wished to discredit the police. The police on this occasion deserved some of the discredit, whatever the truth about the actual striking of the blow, because of their lack of frankness during the inquiry and at the inquest.

The media coverage of the incident, though generally not hostile to the police, was properly investigative, and fair. The National Council for Civil Liberties carried out its own inquiry[15] and *Socialist Worker* made the most of its chances to pursue its campaign. Posters were printed showing individual policemen as wanted for murder, though the Director of Public Prosecutions had already examined the evidence and decided to make no charges. Generally, however, the media coverage of Southall should result in the police being more careful with their orders and their control of such incidents, which can only be of benefit both to the community and to the police themselves. Whether the SWP will welcome this is a question more relevant to the next chapter.

Before the inquest was completed, however, the BBC took the controversial decision to make one of their 'Open Door' programmes available to the Southall Campaign Committee. The idea of this series is to give access to the screen to minority groups who make and edit their own programmes. On this occasion the group made a number of unsubstantiated allegations against the police. The BBC offered the police another 'Open Door' programme which they could edit, to reply to the charges. This, however, was an empty offer since the police could not edit or make specific statements on a programme on a subject which might result in criminal charges in which they would present the evidence for prosecution.

Mr Eldon Griffiths MP, the parliamentary adviser to the Police Federation, commented in a published letter to the BBC: 'It is one thing to broadcast strongly held opinions and quite another to allow your screens to be used deliberately to smear the Police Service and by doing so to inflate racial hatred.'

The question of whether the media, and the BBC in particular, are used in this way is the subject of the next chapter.

6 Reporting the Police

A CONCERTED ATTACK?

The police enjoy the highest public regard of any profession in Britain, with the possible exception of doctors. After a comprehensive three-year survey published in 1975, Dr William Belson recorded proof of the quite remarkable relationship between the Metropolitan Police and the public in London. The heart of his report was a series of multiple choice questions one of which, for example, asked respondents whether they respected the police 'a lot' or 'quite a lot' or 'not very much' or 'not at all'. Counting the first two answers as 'Yes' and the other two as 'No' and recording the number in the top class in each case, his principal finding may be summarized as follows: [1]

Question	Two top categories	Top category
Do you respect the police?	Yes, 98%	A lot, 73%
Do you trust the police?	Yes, 90%	Completely, 30%
Do you like the police?	Yes, 93%	Very much, 31%
Are you satisfied with the police?	Yes, 96%	Very, 61%

These summary questions were reinforced by about 300 other questions asked of a sample of 1200 adults. The first three questions were also asked of 500 London teenagers with surprisingly similar results: 94 per cent 'respected', 83 per cent 'trusted' and 85 per cent 'liked' the police. It is unlikely that any other police service in the world could match these figures.

Yet Eldon Griffiths, parliamentary adviser to the Police Federation, whose comments on the Southall 'Open Door' programme were quoted in the previous chapter, had this to say in the House of Commons in May 1980:

> . . . I believe that we are in the presence of a concerted campaign in the fringes of politics, in the media and occasionally in

this House, to denigrate the police service. There have been attempts to depict the police as brutal beaters up and even killers of persons in custody, as Cossacks deployed by the Government to beat back honest trade unions, as racialists, as corrupters and as fascists. No organ of opinion in this country has done more to disseminate and endorse these mendacities than the BBC.

THE POLICE AND THEIR ENEMIES

Is there a 'concerted attack'? How much of the criticism is justified and how much exaggerated? It is predictable that extremist organizations wish to denigrate the police, but are all those who seek to do so extreme? Do the media, and especially the BBC, consciously or unconsciously contribute to this denigration?

The figures in Dr Belson's table suggest that over 90 per cent of the adult and teenage population of London were generally pro-police six years ago. More recent (but less comprehensive)[2] polls suggest that this figure may have fallen, but only slightly — perhaps to 85 per cent. Looking at it from the other side, if these figures are correct it means that six years ago 10 per cent and today perhaps 15 per cent of the public, are hostile to the police.

Who are these 10 to 15 per cent? Obviously they include the criminal world; they include those teenagers who become delinquent, as vandals or pilferers, and others who rebel against the system as punk rockers, mods or skinheads; they include a worrying proportion of young blacks in high immigrant inner-city areas; and they include a small minority of university students and graduates, some of whom overlap the punk philosophy, and whose main reasons for denigrating the police are political rather than social. This last group contains most of the ones who are articulate in their hostility (i.e. reasoned argument as distinct from mere abuse); they therefore aim to speak for the others, because they feel that no one else will, and because it gives them a wider base.

In the previous chapter the two main sources of social conflict most commonly exploited for political purposes were identified as industrial problems (especially unemployment) and race. With a few exceptions,[3] not many trade union leaders try to arouse their members against the police, whom they generally regard as fellow members of the working class. Most trade union members probably subscribe to the majority attitude towards the police recorded in the Belson Report. The leadership of unemployed workers by 'graduate godfathers' − as, for example, in the Hendon incident described in the previous chapter − has been much more vicious but that leadership is rarely followed. Arousing the antipathy of racial minorities against the police, as at Lewisham and Southall, is much more common.

This antipathy is not difficult to arouse. Black teenagers with nothing to do, and feeling that the majority community is prejudiced against them, are inevitably tempted to turn to pilfering or malicious damage. The more they do so, the stronger becomes the prejudice against them and the less ready people are to offer them jobs. Their crime rate grows with their resentment. The provocative slogan for the Lewisham NF march − '80% of the muggers are black, 85% of the victims are white' − was taken from published police statistics. The police respond by increasing their patrolling of the high crime areas which are the black areas, and as a result are inevitably accused of leaning on the blacks. Young policemen become the butt for taunts and abuse so their own resentment grows too. Some overreact. So the vicious circle develops.

Community relations workers, usually themselves black, co-operate with police Community Relations Officers to restrain this deterioration but all their work can be set at naught by a few incidents in which a small number of coloured youths or a small number of policemen − or both − are to blame.[4]

The Institute of Race Relations, surprisingly in view of its name, does much to exacerbate the problem. Their Race and Class Pamphlet No. 6, *Black People Against the Police* (1979) is a good example of their work. With this kind of lead, it is not surprising that a conference of 100 leaders of 40 or 50 Asian and West Indian organizations in June 1980 called upon the black population to refuse to take part in community liasion schemes or to co-operate with the police in any way.[5] Such calls inevitably increase the hostility of the white majority and increase its solidarity with the police but do no good to race relations. The National Council for Civil Liberties, which generally fills a useful role as a watchdog to guard against police excesses, does not help when it takes a consistently hostile attitude toward the police in the matter of race relations. The NCCL report of the Unofficial Committee of Enquiry, *Southall 23 April 1979*, reports violence by demonstrators and violence by police with a very different bias.[6] Apart from printing a statement made in Parliament by the Home Secretary and a Memorandum placed by him in the Library of the House, the only evidence they called appeared to be hostile to the police.[7] It is hard to believe that the entire population of Southall sympathized with the SWP, the ANL and the Asian and West Indian demonstrators and that none had any sympathy for the police who suffered so many injuries in keeping the NF and the demonstrators apart. Suppressing their views could only increase their hostility towards the blacks, even if it had the rather bleak dividend of increasing their support for the police.

Can these things be regarded as part of a 'concerted attack' on the police? Clearly those who wish to supplant parliamentary democracy will wish to do their best to erode the good relations between the police and the public, since this is the main source of police strength in maintaining the rule of law, and the rule of law is the primary bulwark of parliamentary democracy. But how many such people are there in Britain, and how effective is their attack? Are they aided by others who, while not necessarily wishing to supplant the democratic system, have other reasons to wish to discredit the police?

NEWS AND CURRENT AFFAIRS REPORTING ON THE POLICE

In the reporting of demonstrations, as in the reporting of political terrorism and crime, the news media are generally sympathetic to the police, once again reflecting the sympathy of the majority of their readers and viewers. This public sympathy is deep-rooted, partly because they see the police as their first line of protection against crime, violence and disruption, and partly because they know that this protection involves the police in a dangerous job. When, for example, the ordinary citizen in the street witnesses a robbery or hears shooting or bombing or the sounds of a riot or a fight, his instinct is to do no more than cautiously satisfy his curiosity and to avoid getting personally involved. The policeman who may be standing near him, however, has to go at once, probably unarmed and if necessary alone, to the heart of the danger. The citizen is well aware of this, even if he has not been on the scene himself. He is reminded of it every time a robbery or a riot — or for that matter, the Balcombe Street or Iranian Embassy siege — is reported on the television news. He has a general feeling of admiration and gratitude and, knowing this, the reporter is loath to alienate his readers by knocking the police.

On the other hand, the 'honest brave policeman' has to do something fairly exceptional if he is to make news. If there is a whiff of corruption or bullying or giving false evidence in court, that does make news. The fact that it is rare makes it the more newsworthy when it occurs. Even Katharine Whitehorn, an *Observer* columnist who is certainly no revolutionary, devoted her weekly column twice in one month (15 June and 13 July 1980) to criticizing the police, initially with the not uncommon middle-class complaint of 'why do they waste their time trapping my friend for a minor speeding offence instead of catching criminals', and then with a series of stories of police harassment, mainly of young people. The police would accurately reply that drivers of fast cars kill more people every year than all the criminals put together; and that even the most hot-headed of policemen is nowhere near as provocative or aggressive to young people (black or white) as some young people are to them. Nevertheless, Katharine Whitehorn is right when she says: 'Our police may still be the best in the world, but I cannot believe that refusing to notice their faults is the best way of making sure they stay that way.'[8]

PICKING OUT THE ROTTEN APPLES

The rotten apple in the basket is news, and healthily so. The trouble is that when the news headline — or still more so the TV camera — focuses on the rotten apple it multiplies it a hundred times. In an earlier chapter it was seen that one minute of violence out of a hundred minutes of peaceful picketing dubbed the whole event as violent — and that the answer lay in fair reporting, however briefly, of the background, to put the incident in perspective. The same applies to the reporting of police excesses or dishonesty. Although the rotten apple gets a hundred times the coverage of the good one, a fair report should leave the reader or viewer aware that there are a hundred good apples for every rotten one. Also, just as the context should show if the violent picket is responding to harassment or injustice, so it should show if the policeman is himself responding to provocation or assault. On the other hand, the corrupt or gratuitously aggressive policeman has no more justification than the gratuitously violent picket, demonstrator or terrorist, and should be just as fearlessly exposed.

The problem lies not so much with the uniformed policeman, whose number can be noted if he transgresses, and whose image is reflected in the 90 per cent public approval recorded in the Belson Report. The plain clothes policeman in the CID, however, while more glamorous, is seldom seen by the public. They have to accept him on trust and, if that trust is eroded, the effect on the rule of law can be very serious.

This problem was pointed out by Lord Devlin in an interesting article commissioned by the *Police Review*.[9] He said that the activities of the CID are known only to the few who see them at work in the criminal courts — but that their image is now slightly but distinctly blemished. In the 1930s and 1940s, it had been very difficult for defence counsel to persuade the court that a policeman was lying. This, says Devlin, has changed:

> Public knowledge is now fed not only by the suspicions conveyed by the professionals but by a trickle of cases in the newspapers involving wicked and dishonest police officers: a minority, the good citizen assures himself; and he is right, but it is enough to pollute.
>
> This is having quite a serious effect on our criminal process. It remains true that the average detective officer is far, far more likely to be upright than crooked. If I were to say that 80% are absolutely sound in all respects, it might be a substantial underestimate. But in a system that operates on 100% with a small discount for the inevitable failures, a drop to 90% or, say, 85% is catastrophic.
>
> For the Defence never has to prove that a policeman is lying; it has only to suggest it as a non-fantastic possibility . . .

These doubts amongst juries set in motion a vicious circle. As juries become more reluctant to convict, the CID policeman is more tempted to lie in order that a man whom he is convinced, or even knows for sure, is guilty shall be convicted. Every time such a lie is unmasked, the doubts of the public, the potential jurors, are increased. There is then a temptation to rely more and more on confessions, the more so since the rules of evidence and procedure make it more and more difficult to secure convictions without a confession. Yet it is well established that some people under interrogation, without the slightest hint of ill-treatment, will after a time sign a confession in order to end the ordeal. To make matters worse, these will usually be the weaker, less educated, less experienced people. The professional criminals will know better than to sign confessions, and they therefore make up the majority of the very large percentage of guilty men who are acquitted – to the growing frustration of the CID, who are then tempted to tell more lies to secure their conviction. This was the basis of the *Law and Order* series of television plays discussed in the next chapter.

The ultimate answer can only be to root out the rotten apples, so that the confidence of juries is restored. In the meantime, however, the result must be that the image will worsen before it gets better. As Devlin says, 'The operations mounted against corruption and the publicity given to them can only increase the belief of juries that something is wrong.'

The media must therefore exercise restraint and balance as well as fearlessness in their disclosure. Failure to disclose, however, is the greater fault in the long run. A policeman who secures an unjust conviction by giving false evidence or who aids and abets crime by corruption, and is not detected, will inject a seed of contempt for the law which will grow into something far more damaging than the exposure and rooting out of his rottenness at the time.

This was clearly the view of Sir Robert Mark when he became Commissioner of the Metropolitan Police in 1972. He at once set about cleaning up the CID, where in some areas corruption had penetrated into higher as well as lower ranks. Crooked policemen were ruthlessly hunted out and convicted. At the same time Sir Robert drew attention, in a famous BBC Dimbleby Lecture, to another sprinkling of rotten apples which did not come under his jurisdiction – the crooked lawyers. 'Experienced and respected metropolitan detectives can identify lawyers in criminal practice who are more harmful to society than the clients they represent.'[10]

He was, of course, primarily attacking the lawyers who unscrupulously exploit the safeguards of the law to enable a very high proportion of guilty men to go free. These safeguards were mainly instituted a century or more ago when most of those accused of crimes were poor, deprived and uneducated, and probably bewildered by the whole procedure of arrest, charge and interrogation. The professional criminal of today does not need these safeguards, and their abuse by crooked lawyers merely encourages further abuse by the police. Sir Robert was arguing for a revision of some of the more outdated safeguards in the interests both of justice and protection of the public.

He was, nevertheless, accused by many in the legal profession – not just the crooked ones – of undermining public confidence in the institutions of the law. He was just as right to do this as he was to root out corrupt policemen. The vigilance against police corruption has continued with Operation Countryman, which was still in progress at the time of writing.

There was, however, some justification for both Sir David McNee (Sir Robert's successor) and the Chief Constable of Greater Manchester, James Anderton, when they suggested that the calculated distortion and exaggeration of rotten apples (real or alleged) was in 1979 and 1980 reaching such proportions that it really could be classed as a 'concerted attack'. Addressing the joint conference of the Association of Chief Police Officers, County Councils and Metropolitan Authorities on 5 June 1980, Sir David McNee said 'A recent tactic has been to take a few unconnected incidents, such as Liddle Towers, James Kelly, Blair Peach and Operation Countryman, mention them in one sentence, ignore the facts in each case and conclude that there is a crisis of confidence in the police.'

Part of this campaign, if it was a campaign, was to seize upon the publication of the fact that 274 people (including Towers and Kelly) had died in police custody in the previous ten years.[11] Organs of the media hostile to the police were careful to exclude the fact that this number was a minute percentage of the total number – four million – who had passed through police custody during that period; that a substantial number of the 274 who died had come into police custody as a direct result of being drunk, sometimes violently so, and some were already on the way to death from alcoholism; and that, in ten years, a very large number of those arrested by the police were violent criminals who had to be overpowered. In this context it was, on reflection, hard to believe that as few as one in 15 000 had died between the time of arrest and the time of either committal to prison or release. To state the ten-year figure without qualification, sometimes even in such terms as 'POLICE KILL 274', can only be described as calculated distortion, and there is little doubt that most of those who did so had the intention of discrediting the police, for no credible ends other than political ones.

7   Television Documentaries and Drama

THE PHOTOGRAPHER AND THE ARTIST

While news and current affairs reporting has generally reflected the public support for the police and for the rule of law, this has not always been the same for television documentaries and drama. Because of their need to grasp the interest of audiences, they have to avoid the humdrum even more than news reporters do, and they therefore reflect a higher proportion of the exceptional. This is not necessarily for political reasons and may simply arise from the instinct of documentary journalists and dramatists to look for drama, if necessary at the expense of literal truth.

The difference can be compared to that between a photographer and an artist. The news and current affairs reporter, like the photographer, records the facts — that is, what is in the viewfinder of his camera, give or take a trick or two. The documentarist or dramatist, like the artist, expresses what he believes to be the truth, which may be very different from a photograph.

The photographer's tricks include focusing on a tiny untypical part of the scene (e.g. a face distorted with hate amongst a friendly crowd); he can deliberately distort (e.g. by making a hand or a nose seem unnaturally large); use light and shade for effect; use a short depth of focus to pick out a face and blur the background; and he can falsify by touching up the negative. (Though at that point he literally becomes a painter!) He can do all of these things to get what he considers to be nearer the truth or he can do them deliberately to lie. The reporter (and, of course, his cameraman) can do just the same.

The artist can, however, do far more than this. He can fairly claim to depict the truth more faithfully than the photographer, on the grounds that the human eye is far more selective than the camera, even with all its tricks. The human eye focuses on one particular object — it may just be the subject's face or even just his curling lip or shifty eye. That and that alone will dominate the message from the eye to the brain. In that way the eye *does* record the truth better than the camera, because the significance of what it sees *is* the curling lip or shifty eye.

The documentarist, and even more so the dramatist, can claim that he tells the truth in the same way; that by picking out the essentials and even exaggerating them, he is presenting the truth in the way the brain is accustomed to receiving it from the eye.

DOCUMENTARIES

Television documentaries used to be much more 'photographic' in that sense than they are now. One of the earliest attempts to depict a profession in a TV documentary was Richard Cawston's *The Lawyers* in 1960. He interviewed about 100 barristers and solicitors in actual locations. There were no actors and no sets. In selecting and editing the film, he aired controversies but made no attempt to question the integrity of the legal profession. He set out simply to show it at work. The critics, the lawyers and the public were uniformly delighted. The public, in particular, were not only interested to learn what lay behind the *mystique* of the law, but were also reinforced in their confidence in a profession they generally assumed to be honest.

The same applied to some of the earlier police documentaries. In March 1975, the BBC presented *Police—Harrow Road*, in which their team was given free access to film what they chose, including the operations room, the charge centre and the cells; they accompanied a PC on the beat, a panda car patrol, a call to a major incident and a drugs raid; and they talked to policemen about the way they worked and their views on violence, corruption, crime and punishment. To quote the *Radio Times* promotion of the programme: 'All the filming captured events as they occurred — nothing was "set up" or created for the cameras.'

Police—Harrow Road, like *The Lawyers*, earned universal acclaim. Sir Robert Mark wrote to thank and to congratulate the BBC. It was watched by 8 million people and the BBC had a highly favourable 'Reaction Index', suggesting that the public enjoyed a guided tour around an institution which they liked and trusted. Sean Day-Lewis wrote 'This was a touching and reasonably de-glamorised documentary from which the police . . . emerged with their credit enhanced.' The *Sunday Times* noted that, in contrast to the picture in some of the BBC's fictional dramas, 'the real police turned out to be . . . big, happy, not very well educated, not too daft blokes, prepared to meet trouble.'

THE POLICE MORALITY PLAYS

Television dramas about the police have ranged from *Dixon of Dock Green* and *Z Cars* to the four *Law and Order* plays first broadcast in 1978 and repeated in 1980.

Dixon of Dock Green began in 1955 and ran for 21 years, ending only when the actor playing its hero, Jack Warner, became too old to continue and had become so identified with the part in the public mind that no one else could have credibly replaced him. Dixon was the epitome of the traditional image of the London bobby, a reassuring and philosophical middle-aged cockney. When a real-life Dixon emerged into the limelight − 41-year-old PC Trevor Lock in the London Iranian Embassy siege in May 1980 − the public took him nostalgically to their hearts. This was what they wanted their policemen to be like.

Z Cars, introduced in 1961, struck a new note. It reflected the change in theatrical fashions. While *Dixon's* loyal audience stuck to him and grew older with Jack Warner, a new and younger audience were looking for something less smug and more earthy. The *Z Cars* policemen were younger, tougher, more sceptical about people and blunter in their manner. The public, as Alan Plater put it, wanted working-class heroes.[1] Realism was the watchword. Policemen were shown dealing with the seamier side of life, and with their less attractive clients − drunks, drug-addicts and dropouts, the homeless and the victims of assault. The policemen themselves were not depicted as saints but as young men leading a hard life, sometimes quarrelling with each other and with their wives under the strain − but always on the side of the right. Like *Dixon of Dock Green*, the *Z Cars* plays were morality plays. Virtue always triumphed in the end. *Softly Softly, Task Force* followed a very similar path and all three series were enormously popular.

Meanwhile, American police series like *Kojak* and *Starsky and Hutch* continued in parallel. British TV audiences watched them by the million, but as fantasy rather than real life. A British series in the American mould, *Target*, initially excited much adverse comment because of its glorification of violence, but few people believed that *Target* bore much relation to real life, any more than they believed in the reality of the Hollywood Western. They were just entertainment. Rightly or wrongly, however, the public did believe that police work really was like *Z Cars* and *Softly Softly*.

THE 'LAW AND ORDER' SERIES

Complacency was somewhat shattered by a series of four television plays first broadcast in 1978 under the series title *Law and Order*. This series was written by Gordon Newman, an experienced crime writer, who had learned a great deal about the criminal world and the CID. In particular he had mastered the jargon. The series was brilliantly written and produced, and had a ring of authenticity. Both this and the *Radio Times* background article about it gave the impression that it had some documentary significance. Indeed, some viewers who switched on late were under the impression that they were watching a documentary about an actual case of wrongful conviction.

The series set out to present an indictment of the entire operation of the law in Britain. The four plays were called *The Villain's Tale*, about a professional criminal, Jack Lynn, *The Detective's Tale*, about a CID Detective Sergeant, *The Brief's Tale*, about a crooked lawyer of the kind depicted in Sir Robert Mark's Dimbleby lecture and finally one about Jack Lynn's treatment after he was convicted, in *The Prisoner's Tale*. Though each play could stand separately on its own, the four made up a saga of how Jack Lynn, who had got away with previous crimes, was framed by the police, betrayed by his crooked solicitor and counsel before a parody of a Judge, committed struggling and shouting abuse to prison on fabricated evidence for a crime he had not committed and there, after a continuous battering from sadistic prison officers, was finally cowed and broken. The last scene shows the once proud and defiant Lynn meekly and subserviently tending the Prison Governor's garden, programmed not to make any more trouble for the remainder of his 14 years inside.

It could have been an outstanding series, moving and dramatic. Though it may prove to have had some long-term effect on public attitudes, the BBC believe that it had little immediate effect on the viewers, probably because it was too polemical. The author aimed to show that, to deal with the constant mendacity of the professional crook and his crooked lawyer, the CID detective had to reply in kind; that if he could not nail the professional criminals for the crimes they had committed he must set them up and put them inside for other people's crimes. Possibly because of the limitations of time in a television play, the picture emerged that virtually *every* CID officer was crooked, barring no holds (physical or otherwise) to secure a conviction, talking out of the side of his mouth to another crooked CID officer or to a crooked lawyer, throughout the play. Virtually every lawyer depicted was crooked and virtually every prison officer brutal, violent and sadistic.

The idea for the plays came from the producer, Tony Garnett, who asked Gordon Newman to write them. Garnett is a brilliant producer, with a strong personal political commitment as illustrated by some of his other productions such as the *Days of Hope* series and *The Spongers*. Whatever the motivation of the author, Tony Garnett's purpose was clear. The most telling review of the *Law and Order* series came from Richard Ingrams,[2] who referred to Tony Garnett's 'urge to use a play or film to make propaganda'. Coming from the Editor of *Private Eye*, this was a significant comment.

Subsequent BBC audience research suggested that public confidence in the integrity of the police and the law had not been significantly eroded by the *Law and Order* series.[3] This research, however, was based upon the immediate reaction of a selected audience under rather artificial conditions, since they knew that they were acting as guinea pigs.

Dramatists stress the importance of dramatic truth, claiming that fantasy can present the truth better than factual accuracy. Whether or not this is so, the producer of the *Law and Order* series went too far. The truth is that there have been too many rotten apples in the CID and some have been caught and convicted by the police themselves, but a series which depicts every apple as a rotten apple has no dramatic truth and the public did not immediately believe it. In the long run, however, the plays will have contributed to the erosion of confidence and the vicious circle described by Lord Devlin.[4]

The author and producer of *Law and Order* were no doubt seeking to depict the truth of *some* investigations, *some* charges and *some* trials. Gordon Newman claimed that every incident in the plays was based on a real incident. Except for some of the prison scenes,[5] this may well have been so. Some people have been framed. Some detectives and lawyers have taken bribes. Some policemen have given false evidence. But to give the impression that every lawyer and every policeman does so all the time really can be described as a calculated attempt to discredit the police and the law.

In a televised discussion after the *Law and Order* series another BBC playwright, Alan Plater, declared the belief that a writer of plays was, almost by definition, going to attack the establishment; that was what he was there for; otherwise he would probably end up writing commercials.[6] If that were true it would be a sad day for drama and for society. Shakespeare does not fit that description, nor do many others amongst the playwrights who have been most popular with audiences. Just as there is a need for a National Council for Civil Liberties and for investigative journalists, so there is a need for a fringe theatre and for writers like Alan Plater and producers like Tony Garnett to challenge the establishment and to expose corruption, cruelty and injustice. It is, however, arrogant to suggest that no one else is fit to tell a story or write a play at all. The box office and audience research give a convincing answer. Concurrently with the showing of *Law and Order*, James Herriot's BBC series *All Creatures Great and Small*,[7] all about vets, based on real life and certainly not anti-establishment, was drawing roughly ten times the audience.

Perhaps the most serious effect of the *Law and Order* series was in the criminal fraternity itself. In the BBC General Advisory Council's debate on the series one of the participants was a QC with long experience of defending professional criminals. He said that they would be greatly encouraged by the series, on the grounds that it would sow doubts in minds of potential jurors as to the fairness and integrity of both the police and the lawyers involved in presenting the case before them. Lord Devlin's remarks bear this out.

One such series would not achieve that effect on its own but the seed it sows can grow. In a paper on *The Reflection in BBC Programmes of the Institutions of Law and Order* prepared for the General Advisory Council in July 1980,[8] the BBC, who were generally defending their record, did draw attention to the marked decline in public confidence in the integrity of the police and the law. The paper said that 'producers play back to society its own confident or not so confident image of the institutions of law and order'. It suggests that Sir Robert Mark's Dimbleby Lecture had more effect in eroding this confidence than the TV dramas and documentaries. Sir Robert Mark's own comment in the TV discussion of such programmes in *The Truth Game* is therefore particularly relevant. He said that the *Law and Order* series was so well done that it seemed like a documentary and that, while such plays should certainly be shown, they should be balanced by the truth. This balance did not lie just in having more morality plays like *Z Cars* but in more *real* documentaries about the police and the institutions of law and order; and that these documentaries should deal with the *real* problems of the police, not just crime but also those arising from inflation, industrial conflict, unemployment, hooliganism, vandalism and racial tension.[9]

8 Disclose or Discredit?

THE DUTY TO DISCLOSE

It has throughout been the theme of this book that the strength and durability of a pluralist society lie in the freedom of its media to investigate and disclose the malpractices which can destroy it, above all corruption, dishonesty, brutality, intimidation, coercion and injustice. When these malpractices occur in the very institutions of the rule of law, it is especially important that they be exposed. The searchlight for such exposure has historically been fiction and drama as often as it has been the reporting of news and comment.

Katharine Whitehorn has put the case for exposure of police harassment, especially of the young, and for exposure of police giving false or exaggerated evidence to secure convictions:

> . . . the point is not just whether this or that injustice can be faulted. The point is that every time something like this happens even trivially, whether the police are half-right or driven beyond endurance or just having a bad day, one of their friends is turned into an enemy.
>
> If I was a revolutionary I would be delighted with all such incidents; I would like nothing better than a hostile, swaggering, aggressive police force — just because so many people would be against them when the crunch came. I'm not, so I worry . . .[1]

The same applies to the deterrent effect of exposure of police overreaction to violence on picket lines and on demonstrations. Some senior police officers have said that they welcome the overt presence of television cameras on such occasions, as they will discourage any young lions there may be amongst police ranks from overreacting.

This produces an interesting contrast in motives. The visible presence of the TV camera may have reverse effects on political demonstrators and the police. It often encourages the demonstrators to act up so as to attract attention and to use violence in order to provoke police reaction which will discredit the police. For this same reason, the sight of the camera restrains the policemen themselves.

The motive of the producer, reporter and cameraman is all important. One experienced TV reporter asks her cameraman to merge into the crowd with a small hand-held camera hidden under a loose anorak. When there is something to film he whisks the camera on to his shoulder and runs it for a few seconds before dropping it back under his anorak and moving elsewhere. This, she feels, gives her true pictures rather than acted ones. On the other hand a cameraman out to discredit either the police or the demonstrators can use precisely the same technique in order to catch either of them using violence when they are unaware that they are being filmed. The visible presence of the camera may thus restrain some people as well as encouraging others to act up.

It is right that violence, both against the police and by the police, should be filmed and exposed. The bias, if any, comes out in the selection and editing of the film. The editor may be out to give a fair picture or to discredit the demonstrators or to discredit the police.

MALICE AND MOTIVATION

Very few BBC or ITV news or current affairs reporters allow themselves to be unduly influenced by any personal political motivation to discredit the police, although a few programmes like Jonathan Dimbleby's *A Force to Reckon With*[2] must raise doubts. There can be no doubt, however, about the political motivation of the Southall Campaign Committee which was given access to television in the 'Open Door' programme about the Southall Riot. In giving air time to a programme as predictably biased as this one, to which the police had no means of reply nor even (as an institution as distinct from named individuals) any means of legal redress the BBC were, to say the least, naive.

The same criticism of the BBC, IBA and ITV companies must be levelled in some of the cases where access is given to writers, directors and producers of TV drama which is patently dishonest and politically motivated. The criteria for selection of a play for production should be not only artistic quality and dramatic impact but also dramatic truth, and the selection of a producer should be based on the trust that his production, like the script, will reflect this dramatic truth. If his record shows that, however good his productions may be, he uses them to promulgate his own political propaganda at the expense of dramatic truth, he should not be given that opportunity. To judge a new producer may be more difficult but, if he proves to have betrayed that trust, he should not be given access to such a mighty medium of communication again.

In his reply to another attack by Mr Eldon Griffiths MP on the BBC for deliberating denigrating the police, the Director-General of the BBC wrote

No broadcaster, nor for that matter newspaperman, will lightly report allegations against the police. We all know that our own professional freedom and independence rest on Parliamentary democracy and the rule of law. But we also know that the enforcement of the law is a matter of legitimate public concern, and that a freedom must be exercised, albeit with care and responsibility, if it is not to invite erosion.

This could hardly be better put. He could with equal truth have said, as a member of the public, that 'our own *personal* freedom and independence rest on parliamentary democracy and the rule of law'.

The community, and those who direct its mass media, must therefore be vigilant in ensuring that the media should not be misused with the intention of attacking that freedom and independence by calculatedly discrediting the rule of law and the police and institutions which preserve it. It is not always easy to distinguish in advance whether a report or comment or programme will have that effect, or whether it will have the salutary effect of strengthening those institutions and the rule of law by exposing and thereby deterring malpractices. In making this distinction the detection of the motive is decisive, and motives may be easier to detect than distortions or inaccuracies.

Part III
Terrorism

9　The IRA and the Media

A HOSTILE ENVIRONMENT

By January 1980 the total number of people killed in the political violence in Northern Ireland since August 1969 had passed 2000. Of those, 327 were British soldiers. The remaining 1673 were virtually all Northern Irish men, women and children, including 230 Ulster part-time volunteer soldiers and policemen and over 1400 other civilians. At least 1000 of these were killed by the Irish Republican Army (IRA). Another 16 000 were injured.[1] Out of a total population of 1½ million, more than one in every hundred, man, woman and child, was either killed or wounded by someone intending to kill or wound, using bomb, bullet or knife.

Yet the conflict in Ireland has been described as 'a propaganda war supported by a shooting war', and the shooting has more often hindered than helped. Far from making the Protestant majority more accommodating, the IRA violence made them more intransigent until, by 1974, the previously powerful section of the Unionist Party which had been willing to share power with the Catholics had lost every one of its seats in Parliament. When British soldiers killed 13 young men during a shoot-out in Londonderry in 1972,[2] contributions to the IRA from the Irish American community quadrupled. Six months later, however, the IRA set off 19 bombs in the main shopping area of Belfast, killing 9 people and wounding many others, whereupon the contributions from USA promptly fell back lower than before and never recovered.

Not surprisingly, the killing sharpened the hostility of the Protestants and Catholics towards each other, but it also made them hostile towards almost everyone else. When the army or police arrested or killed a Catholic, no matter what the circumstances, IRA propaganda naturally made the most of the chance to arouse passions amongst the Catholic community. Similarly, if a Protestant gunman was killed, his community cursed the army, whose success in preventing other incidents or in combating the

87

IRA, even if reported, would get little compensating credit. Indeed the army was attacked for being 'soft with the IRA'. Journalists suffered too. Criticism of any kind drew an angry response from the community criticized, but passed unnoticed by the other community. Each always accused the media of irresponsibility or a hostile bias or both. 'He who is not with us is against us.'

The extremist movements on both sides have had an enormous advantage over the police and the army in the propaganda war. Immediately an incident of any kind has occurred, journalists have been intensely and competitively hungry for news. Any account from any source in time for the next deadline would be better than none. Since the IRA have initiated most of the incidents, they have been able to prepare highly coloured stories in advance, needing only minor change and embellishment. Moreover, these stories could be told by ready-briefed 'eye-witnesses' and, however false, inaccurate or exaggerated, the stories have not in any way tied the IRA, who were later able to issue a revised account without any need to explain the difference. The army or police, however, have had to live with any statement made by any soldier, policeman or junior officer and, if this later had to be corrected, they paid a heavy price in the credibility of the whole force. They have therefore had to be cautious and their version has usually come a bad second in the race for the news, often missing the deadline for the final news bulletin which carried the IRA story unchallenged. Examples of this will be discussed later.

An important factor in this equation, especially in the British press, was that Northern Ireland has offered an excellent proving ground for giving young journalists a chance to make their names. This has given them an incentive to make their stories as lively and original as possible. This in turn has led many of them to establish clandestine contacts with members of terrorist movements of one or both sides. This was obviously a dangerous game. Any suspicion of spying or betrayal might have had fatal results.[3] On the other hand, a reputation for readiness to transmit propaganda, whether with intent or with gullibility, would lead to development of the contact, more information and thence more original and exciting articles. The temptation was intense and some journalists, with no personal sympathy for the IRA, were unable to resist it.

Opinions differ on how far the media have encouraged or inflamed violence and how far they have shocked people into restraint by 'bringing the blood into the living room' on colour TV. Live radio reports of riots in progress have undoubtedly brought out more local supporters from both sides in the immediate locality to join in — so much so that the BBC was urged to place a ban on live reporting of violence.[4] There is good reason to believe that the immense publicity given to the INLA after the murder of Airey Neave, MP, was a major factor in the IRA's decision to match it by murdering Earl Mountbatten.[5] On the other hand, in the early days, a British Army Brigade Commander in Belfast observed that the reporting of vicious violence did arouse such revulsion that the hotheads of both sides on the streets were led to be more careful in the image they were creating, even amongst their own community.[6] Nevertheless, this was in a period of rioting rather than terrorism, and has probably not applied in more recent years — with a few notable exceptions such as the IRA mass bombing of central Belfast on 'Bloody Friday' in July 1972, when the vivid television pictures of dead and wounded women and children so shocked the Catholic communities in Belfast and Londonderry that, when the British Army decided to reoccupy the 'no-go' areas two weeks later, the IRA withdrew in advance, knowing that resistance would attract no support from the local population.

THE USE OF THE MEDIA BY THE IRA

In 1922, an official British War Office Record noted that 'in one department, namely publicity, it [Sinn Fein] was unrivalled. This department was energetic, subtle and exceptionally skilful in mixing truth, falsehood and exaggeration and was perhaps the most powerful and least fought arm of the Sinn Fein forces.'[7]

The IRA has maintained this skill. Except during the 1919–21 Rebellion itself, it has never enjoyed more than minority support either in the South or North of Ireland and it has been outlawed by every government in Dublin since 1922, including those of its own parent political party, Fianna Fail, since it first came to power under De Valera in 1932. Except in a few isolated localities such as the Ardoyne in Belfast and parts of Londonderry and South Armagh, its popular support for more than half a century has been measured in single figure percentages. Its propaganda arm (Sinn Fein) has therefore always been more vital to its survival, and hence more effective, than its combat arm.

The Provisional Sinn Fein (unlike the IRA) has remained legal and overt in Britain, Northern Ireland and the Republic. It runs a head office in Dublin and has a Northern headquarters in the Falls Road, Belfast. It has also, since the 1976 'ceasefire' agreement with the British Government (still technically in force), operated 'incident centres' in the main Catholic areas in Belfast (e.g. in the Ardoyne and New Lodge Road) which are really information centres, providing local broadsheets supporting the Provisional IRA and denouncing everyone else from the Official IRA to the British Army. Provisional Sinn Fein also publishes its own newspaper, *An Phoblacht*.

In presenting a story to local, national or world media a Provisional Sinn Fein spokesman has always had to bear in mind some nine different audiences, each with different perceptions, different reactions and different influences on events. First, he has had to consider the effect of the story on the morale of IRA members and on their loyal supporters in hard-core districts in Belfast, Londonderry and South Armagh. Second were those who might be wavering between support of the Provisionals or rival groups such as the Official IRA or the Irish Republican Socialist Party (IRSP) and its military wing the Irish National Liberation Army (INLA). Third were the great mass of other Northern Irish Catholics who, though sharing the aim of a United Ireland, were opposed to violence. Fourth were their mirror image, the moderate majority of the Protestant community, who might be aroused from their moderation if provoked or who could, the IRA hoped, be cowed and demoralized by IRA successes. Fifth were the hard-line protestant 'loyalists' and their paramilitary vigilantes or terrorists, who were targets for demoralization like the members of a rival football team, to be convinced that they were doomed to defeat. Sixth were the British public, who had to be sickened of the war and persuaded that it was not worth expending their soldiers' lives or their money in Northern Ireland at all. Seventh were the mass of the population in the Republic of Ireland most of whom would wish to see reunification one day, but wished to have nothing to do with the IRA. Eighth were the Irish American community, four times more numerous than the combined population of Northern and Southern Ireland, and containing a proportion who were willing to provide money or guns to the IRA — a proportion which could be multiplied by rousing propaganda. Ninth were the rest of the world, ranging from Libyans and Palestinians ready to provide arms or money, to countries largely unaware of the Irish problem and which could be easily misled by propaganda.

Certain media have been aimed largely at one or two groups and are unlikely to be seen by others. *An Phoblacht*, for example, would be circulated almost exclusively amongst dedicated Provisional supporters in Northern and Southern Ireland or in the USA. London papers, Dublin papers and New York papers have had obviously different readerships but if any story could be got into any national newspaper or (better still) television network it would have a good chance of repetition so as to reach members of all nine groups. A skilled propagandist would bear this in mind in slanting his story for maximum productive and minimum counter-productive effect. As Lord Annan stated in his report about television: [8]

Terrorism feeds off publicity: publicity is its main hope of intimidating government and the public: publicity gives it a further chance for recruitment. The acts terrorists commit are each minor incidents in their general campaign to attract attention to their cause. No democracy can tolerate terrorism because it is a denial of the democratic assumption that injustice can, in time, be put right through discussion, peaceful persuasion and compromise. By killing and destroying, the terrorists are bound to extort publicity — and hence one of their ends — because such news will be reported.

The IRA were well aware of this. Maria McGuire, one of the few university graduates who joined the Provisional IRA (though she soon left it), showed in her book the importance they attached to propaganda.[9] Most news reporters confirm this. Bombs were frequently timed to coincide with the evening rush hour when they would cause maximum impact. This had the added advantage that they would get a mention in the six o'clock TV news. The same applied to shooting incidents in which the aim was to involve the army; these would be timed so that the IRA's pre-drafted story, amended as necessary, could be issued to the press in time for news bulletin or newspaper deadlines — but carefully calculated to ensure that police or army accounts would be too late. The Provisional Sinn Fein hired a telex machine from the Post Office (which cannot withhold it from them so long as they remain legal and pay the bill) as an additional weapon in this race for the news. In July 1974 an analysis of 60 bomb explosions showed that over 80 per cent were timed to obtain maximum coverage on television news.[10]

Some of the most productive publicity for the IRA and the INLA has come from clandestine interviews broadcast on British television, with the co-operation, from various motives, sincere, naive or self-seeking, of British journalists. These interviews are discussed later in Chapter 11.

The prime skill of the IRA, however, has lain in organizing their 'supporters', willing or coerced, on the scene of an incident. Tugwell describes it thus:

> The Provisionals drilled the Catholics to cover up whenever security forces shot an insurgent. Almost invariably such an event set this procedure in motion. The man's weapon was spirited away. The victim was taken where he could be cleared of any forensic or other evidence indicating the use of a firearm. 'Eye witnesses' were briefed and presented to news reporters. Their evidence hardly ever varied: the civilian had been unarmed, innocent of any offence, and the soldier's shot had been unwarranted. In short, the army had committed murder. This, it was hoped, would discredit the army and deter soldiers from opening fire on terrorists in future.
>
> Reporters are accustomed to confused and contradicting versions of any incident. It is one of their skills to sort out truth from error. Few newsmen could bring themselves to believe that every civilian was lying. In consequence the army's case, often resting on a single witness, was routinely called into question. Only after many months in Northern Ireland did one experienced reporter (Tony Geraghty of the *Sunday Times*) conclude: 'I speak as someone of Irish extraction on both sides, yet even I am surprised on occasions at the instant and expert mendacity to which journalists, and no doubt other interested parties such as the police and security forces, are treated in episodes of this sort.'[11]

Another experienced reporter, Martin Bell of the BBC, however, described two occasions on which the IRA failed to achieve this. In the first case, in the Ardoyne, a young man had been killed

. . . and it had been fairly clear that he had been carrying a gun because as soon as one got there with one's camera there was deep hostility by the local people whereas if in fact he was an innocent bystander they would say 'come in and see what these bastards have done to us.' But no, I was chased out at gunpoint by the IRA. They had not time to manufacture a fancy story. A lot of the disputed incidents when you actually look at the case histories tended to take place the maximum possible distance from where the media was.

The other example concerned the incident in Andersonstown which resulted in the foundation of the Peace Movement, when three young children were killed by an IRA vehicle fleeing from an army patrol which had fired and hit the driver. Martin Bell found an eight-year-old boy who had seen it happen.

I put him on camera and he gave me a coherent account of what had happened. Believable as it only can be coming from the 'mouths of babes and sucklings' — no-one could have told him what to say — he just said it, and this I subsequently learned caused an awful lot of offence to the IRA because it precluded them from making their own version . . . one then had to ask oneself 'is this fellow going to be victimised?' and I figured that even the IRA wouldn't have it in for an eight-year-old kid.[12]

THE PROBLEM OF *SUB JUDICE*

Another factor of great assistance to the terrorist in the UK is the law on contempt of court and especially the virtual blackout of further comment on a case when it becomes *sub judice*. This was well illustrated in the aftermath of 'Bloody Sunday' in 1972, when the IRA and their sympathizers had been able to present a totally false story of British army parachutists firing upon the marchers in a peaceful demonstration which the government and security forces were barred from refuting because of a decision to hold a judicial inquiry.

The actual events began with a Catholic Civil Rights march through the Bogside which was diverted by a series of army road blocks from entering the Protestant area of Londonderry. A group of about 150 boys broke away and attacked one of the road blocks in William Street. The marchers had meanwhile turned off into the Bogside and gathered for a meeting about 500 yards away behind some high blocks of flats.

When a helicopter observer reported that the tail of the march was safely beyond the buildings, the army reserve (the 1st Battalion of the Parachute Regiment) was ordered to arrest the boys attacking the army road block and chased them across William Street into an area of open ground. While they were catching the boys (they arrested about 70 of the 150) the parachutists were fired upon both from the flats and from a barricade manned by the IRA in the road beside them. The soldiers returned the fire and during the battle an eye-witness behind the flats reported that about 50 more armed IRA reinforcements came in by car and joined in. Forensic evidence later revealed that a roughly equal number of rounds (a little over 100) was fired by the two sides.[13] Thirteen young men were killed, almost all along a line through the barricade and around the buildings either side of it (described by one of the counsel in the judicial inquiry as a military line of defence). There were six actually on the barricade itself.[14] As usual, their weapons were removed by their comrades as they withdrew. The IRA, however, had failed to hit anyone with any of their shots, so they were able to put out the story — on the spot — that the soldiers had fired upon a crowd of unarmed marchers.

This was immediately denied by the army — and was, of course, later proved by the evidence to be a total fabrication — but the government decision, the day after the event, to order a judicial inquiry made the case *sub judice* and thereby banned the publication of their evidence until many weeks later. By this time, however, the damage was done. The highly emotive accounts of soldiers firing on the crowd went unanswered apart from the initial bare denials, and so were largely believed, especially amongst the Irish community in the USA, to the enormous benefit of the IRA funds.

This effect was increased by a number of British reporters who had themselves heard only one side of the story. Some were avowedly sympathetic to the Sinn Fein cause (even though they avoided open support for the IRA) but others were honestly misled, and their reports, repeated by American and European newspapers, were valuable and encouraging for the IRA. As a result, the continuing violence during that year (1972) reached a peak of nearly double that in any other year of the conflict.[15]

10 The Police and the Army in Northern Ireland

THE RUC AND ARMY PRESS OFFICES

When the clashes between the Catholic Civil Rights marchers and the Reverend Ian Paisley's Protestant demonstrators began in 1968, the Royal Ulster Constabulary had no press office. Moreover, the RUC was geared to its traditional role of protecting the Province against the IRA. Its intelligence organization provided plenty of information about the IRA and, through their mutual connections, about the Civil Rights Association (later known as NICRA) but very little about the self-proclaimed Protestant 'loyalists', who they had always assumed were 'loyal' to the Crown and to the police. When the Protestant campaign of deliberate obstruction, confrontation and later of violence against NICRA began, the RUC were quite unprepared for it, and especially for the public relations task of handling the flood of complaints from the two sides, both of which resented anything the police might do which afforded any protection whatever to the rights of the other side or which inhibited any action, however violent or provocative, by their own side.

The RUC's first crisis of confidence occurred on 5 October 1968 when there was a violent confrontation between Civil Rights marchers and an RUC cordon deployed to prevent them from entering the Protestant area of Londonderry. The RUC drew their truncheons and there were some dramatic television films of policemen chasing and clubbing demonstrators. These were screened worldwide, and press pictures and reports were equally emotive, some describing the RUC action as a 'police riot'. The RUC, having no press office, failed to answer these allegations or even to give their side of the story. The result was serious and lasting damage to their image and, consequently, to their morale.

It was not until late 1969, when the violence on the streets had become lethal, that the RUC formed its information service, which has since become highly efficient. The RUC press office policy was to minimize the advantage enjoyed by the instigators of violence by getting the facts, accurately and honestly, to the journalists as quickly as possible, with a professional awareness of deadlines. Given such facts in time, most experienced journalists would trust a report from such an official source more than those of others because they knew that the official source would seek accuracy because of the heavy price they would pay if the report later proved to be wrong.

The army had its own public relations department in being when it was called out into the streets in August 1969. This was composed of a mixture of professionals (ex-journalists), civilian PR staff, officers temporarily seconded from combat units whose experience helped them to interpret both the events and the effects the reporting of them would have in the streets, and other army staff who specialized permanently in PR. The press office at Army HQ in Lisburn in 1969, however, was initially geared to answering enquiries from journalists and promoting the army's image by sympathetic 'local boy stories' and was not really prepared to cope with the professional propaganda campaign which was launched against it (with strong financial backing from the Irish American community), in the summer of 1970.

Within a year or so, the army had developed a positive approach to the media and founded an 'Information Policy' department, initially under an experienced Colonel from the Parachute Regiment, Maurice Tugwell.[1] His job was not merely to react to the media — or to events — but to take a positive initiative in presenting the news to the best advantage for the security forces. Since the IRA killed three civilians for every soldier they killed, individual incidents well interpreted could have — and did have — a very damaging effect on the IRA's image. There is little doubt that this was the greatest deterrent to IRA violence, contributing to the sharp reduction in the numbers killed after 1972. Still more important, in the long run, was the decline in local support for the IRA amongst the Catholic population. In 1971–2, it was fair to assume that 10 per cent of the Northern Catholics sympathized with the IRA and that in hard-core areas the pressure of local public opinion ensured that all doors were open to them. By 1974, the great majority even in hard-core areas of Belfast kept their doors bolted and barred against all uninvited visitors including the

IRA, who were at best tolerated, sometimes feared and generally hated.

THE GLOVER REPORT

By 1978, this disaffection had become so widespread that the IRA could no longer rely on the people even in previously safe areas, where the desire to be rid of the shooting and the bombing induced many to give information to the security forces provided that they were confident that they would not be exposed as informers. As a result, the IRA had to abandon their traditional military structure in which the local battalion and company officers – CO, adjutant, quartermaster, etc. – had been well known to the inhabitants, from whom they could co-opt volunteers for bombing operations or attacks on police stations or army posts. The identities and movements of these IRA officers had increasingly been leaked to the RUC who could then watch them and build up evidence for conviction, so they reorganized into a more secret revolutionary cell structure in which each group of company officers formed an Active Service Unit (ASU) – an organization which they had long used for clandestine operations in Britain. When formed in Northern Ireland, these ASUs were more secure but, because they curtailed their direct links with the people, their popular support declined still further. The people preferred to keep out of the fighting, and to keep it away from their own home streets, if they possibly could.

This reorganization became public knowledge in May 1979 when a secret army document which became known as the Glover Report[2] was stolen by a Post Office worker from the registered mail and communicated first to the Provisional IRA and then to the whole world press.[3] The Glover Report analyzed the reorganization and assessed the IRA strength in men and weapons. It also deduced that this clandestine organization would be harder to find and therefore that the IRA would probably survive for some years.

The press understandably interpreted this as a pessimistic document, and made little reference to the decline in popular support for the IRA which had caused the reorganization and the further loss of influence over the public which would result from it. Since the document was too long to publish in full, the press summaries greatly encouraged the IRA and their supporters. This could have been mitigated if the army had been quicker to release an accurate summary. Not surprisingly, however, they were quite unprepared for the sudden revelation of a stolen secret document. As it was, the boost to IRA morale had the result of increasing their killing rate in 1979, reversing a steady decline for several years past — though it still remained less than a quarter of its peak 1972 rate.

SOLDIERS AND POLICEMEN ON TELEVISION

Another constructive change arising from the introduction of the army's Information Policy staff was the decision late in 1971 to relax the restrictions on soldiers answering questions from reporters. Soldiers were still forbidden to express views in public on policy or politics but they were told that they could now describe and discuss, in front of the camera on the scene, the immediate incident in which they had been involved. This bold decision was rewarded with an overwhelming balance of advantage. Corporals in charge of patrols, in particular, came through on television into the living room far better than generals or colonels. If a corporal did say anything inadvisable, it did less harm than if his colonel had said it, because the viewer knew well enough that corporals do not make policy. The image of the young corporal, calmly and professionally sorting out the mess after a violent incident or facing provocation with restraint and good humour, had a tremendous impact on the viewer. It was particularly effective in countering the 'jackboot' image which hostile journalists will try to project about the army or the police. These were by no means confined to those who supported the IRA as such. There will always be a number of journalists who, for a more general political purpose, try to attack the 'establishment' and all its works and will seize any chance to discredit soldiers or policemen. For some of these journalists working for British newspapers or television, the conflict in Northern Ireland provided superb opportunities for selective pictures of British soldiers using force. Their attempts to depict the soldier as a bully, however, were largely negated for the ordinary viewer of television news when someone like the boy next door appeared on the screen in the living room doing a difficult and dangerous job in a compassionate and sensible way. There are important lessons here. Television news reporters report what they see, and there is little time or inclination to slant it. When those responsible for combating violence have something good to be seen, they should try to put it in front of the camera.

The RUC, however — like the police in Britain — have seldom been able to do this. The police are responsible for prosecutions, and PCs on the spot are likely to be key witnesses, so even a brief remark in front of the TV camera can lead to the overturning of a charge or the quashing of a conviction. Young policemen could have had the same impact on the TV screen as young soldiers, but their insulation from the camera denied them this chance — with the result that the attempt to discredit the RUC in Britain, Northern Ireland and all over the world, had more success than the campaign to discredit the British Army. This was made easier by the fact that fear of victimization of their families deters many Catholics from joining the RUC, with the result that it is disproportionately Protestant, so it is easy to make accusations of prejudice more credible.

Nevertheless, both the army and the RUC learned that it was better to co-operate with journalists (unless there was a strong reason in individual cases to distrust them) than to try to keep them at arms length. Journalists need news and, if blocked by the authorities, will find a way round them. Despite the advantage of the IRA in being able to prepare witnesses at incidents they instigate, the army and the police have, in the end, far greater ability to help journalists — and especially those with camera crews — to get to where the action is; they control the roads and have operational radio networks; they wear uniforms, wield authority and (unlike the clandestine terrorists) can talk freely and openly without prejudicing their own security. Sometimes, exasperated officers or NCOs, coping with a crisis, with blazing buildings and dead and wounded people around them would tell reporters to get out of their hair, but more often they did as they were trained to do and helped the media to get the truth.

THE CONFLICTING DEMANDS OF SPEED AND ACCURACY

Sometimes, however, the desire of the army to give the press the facts without delay could lead to trouble. Until the individual soldier or the press office could be sure that the facts reported were accurate, it was better to make no comment even if — as was discussed earlier — this has meant that the first news bulletin or newspaper report might contain a false account by the IRA without challenge. The damage done by an inaccurate official statement is far greater as was illustrated by an incident in 1978, in which an innocent 16-year-old boy, John Boyle, was shot dead by two soldiers who had 'staked out' an arms cache in a graveyard near a farmyard in Dunloy.[4]

The cache had in fact been reported by the Boyle family to the RUC who at once asked the SAS to stake it out. This was a normal procedure and only a few weeks previously an SAS team had successfully shot four IRA men in a similar stake-out operation in Belfast.

The Boyle family was warned by the RUC to keep away from the arms cache but unfortunately this warning did not reach them until after the SAS stake-out had been established, and the young John Boyle, unaware that the soldiers were there, went to have a look at it. He picked up an Armalite rifle from the cache. The presumption is that at this moment he caught sight of one of the two soldiers and gave an involuntary start. Since the gun was pointing their way and they assumed that he was about to shoot, the soldiers did not wait to shout a challenge but opened fire immediately and killed him.

This is the kind of split-second decision which a soldier has to take when faced with a man carrying a gun in Northern Ireland. It is not easy in this context to tell whether a young man is 16 or 19 and the IRA have regularly used teenagers to do the shooting. One can blame the delay in warning the family but one can hardly blame the soldiers — and they were later cleared of blame by the court.

The incident occurred at 10.22 a.m. on 11 July 1978. The soldiers assumed that the dead boy was an IRA member. Just beforehand a tractor had stopped outside the graveyard and they thought that the boy had come from it, so arrested another man who was driving the tractor, and a third man who arrived on the scene was also arrested. Both were later handed over to the RUC.

The army press office, aware of the stake-out but otherwise having only the bare facts (one man shot and two arrested beside an IRA arms cache) answered press enquiries with a short statement that 'at approximately 10.22 this morning near Dunloy a uniformed military patrol challenged three men. One man was shot; two men are assisting police enquiries. Weapons and explosives have been recovered.' Since two men were arrested they assumed that a challenge would have been given before the soldiers fired. Later, however, after officers had arrived on the scene and had learned fuller details from the soldiers, the army press office issued a second account, which included a correction: 'In our first report we said a challenge was given; on detailed investigation we find this was not so. It was impracticable for the soldiers to issue a warning before firing as the man was ten yards from them pointing a rifle at them.'

There was a wave of outraged criticism in the press. Even the Reverend Ian Paisley was reported as calling the army 'dishonest'.[5] The tragic irony that the boy was a member of the family which had reported the cache made the incident all the more poignant. The press was almost united in its criticism, in speculation about what had really happened and in casting doubt on the credibility of army statements generally.[6]

The Secretary of State for Northern Ireland sent a personal message of sympathy to the family and promised a full investigation by the police. This made the case *sub judice* so that the army, as in the case of Bloody Sunday, was unable to issue any further statements explaining what had actually happened or to refute any of the sometimes wildly inaccurate conjecture about the incident. Since the army's standing instructions to soldiers require them to issue a challenge unless there is an immediate risk to their own or other lives, and the boy was in fact not threatening their lives, there was a *prima facie* case to answer and the two soldiers were charged with murder. The allegations therefore stood unanswered for a whole year until the soldiers had been tried and acquitted of the charge in July 1979. Only then was the army commander, Lieutenant-General Sir Timothy Creasey, able to issue a statement, saying that he had never doubted the good faith of the soldiers in taking their split-second decision, but the army accepted that they must be subject to the full scrutiny of the law and that they had therefore to 'live with the constraints made by the rules of *sub judice* which have to be accepted, often in the face of wild allegations'.[7]

During these twelve months *sub judice*, however, the unchallenged allegations and the attacks on the army's credibility in the light of its initially incorrect statement did immense damage. This drove home the lesson that it would have been better to make no statement at all until there had been time to ensure that it was accurate. When the first statement proved wrong, the frank admission and correction within a few hours, with no attempt to cover it up, at least prevented the damage from being worse than it was. The fact that the soldiers faced public trial for murder also proved better than words that they were just as answerable to the law as any other citizens. There can be very few countries in the world where this would have happened and this point was not lost on the press in the end, but by then much damage had been done.

The overriding principle for an army or police press office must be to tell the truth, whether this is palatable or not. A negative argument is that this is only common sense because the truth (in a society with a free press) is bound to come out in the end. There are, however, two positive arguments which are much stronger than this. First (as illustrated by the Dunloy incident) the reputation of the official press office for telling the truth is a far greater asset in the long run than any advantage which might come from hushing up an embarrassing incident; and secondly, in the great majority of cases, the truth is overwhelmingly favourable to the security forces and damaging to the terrorists.

In Northern Ireland, the IRA have set off literally thousands of bombs (over 1000 in 1972 and still as many as 400 in 1979). A very great number of the 1000 civilians they have killed were the indiscriminate victims of these bombs including large numbers of women and children. Though the army have sometimes made mistakes (as at Dunloy) it has not killed people indiscriminately. The public does not like indiscriminate killing and Catholics dislike it as much as Protestants.

The IRA and the Protestant paramilitaries carry out clandestine sectarian and factional assassinations. There were 113 such assassinations in 1975, 49 of the victims being Protestant and 64 Catholic. Though these too have declined, there were still 31 victims in 1979 and the assassinations continue. This is, in effect, a form of secret capital punishment. By contrast, the state does not use capital punishment. Unless shot in battle the worst that an IRA man has to fear is imprisonment, and that only after a public trial. The public does not like secret assassinations, and the more it learns of the truth the less it likes the IRA and the paramilitaries.

Finally, 99 per cent of the public in Northern Ireland want peace and the clearing of the gunmen and bombers from the streets. They know well enough that in almost every case (Dunloy again being an exception) it is the IRA or the Protestant terrorists who shoot first. If they both went away the shooting would end.

Journalists, as has repeatedly been illustrated in this book, are motivated mainly by a desire to get a response from their regular or potential readers and viewers; they therefore reflect the preferences of their public more often than they attempt to impose their own personal political views upon it. With the obvious exception of readers of papers like *An Phoblacht* and a few British journals such as *Socialist Worker* and *Socialist Challenge* with tiny circulations, the vast majority of both Irish and British readers would rather see soldiers and policemen on the streets than gunmen and bombers, even those with whom they share a political aim.

Because of its 'man-bites-dog' angle, the rare occasions when soldiers kill innocent people (Dunloy again) get vastly more than their share of coverage. Similarly, a soldier or policeman overreacting in a riot is more newsworthy than the sadly familiar routine cavalcade of clandestine assassinations and 'disciplinary knee-cappings' by the IRA. Nevertheless, the truth of all the incidents combined is so damaging to the terrorists and beneficial to the security forces that the more widely it is disseminated the better. Because the terrorists are clearly selective in their propaganda, the army and RUC press offices have actually gained by the contrast when they give the news to the press 'warts and all'. The truth prevailed and was believed.

THE ETHICS OF REPORTING VIOLENCE IN NORTHERN IRELAND

Richard Francis, on completing five years as BBC Controller Northern Ireland Region, gave a lecture at Chatham House in which he analyzed the dilemma of the journalist in reporting conflict. During his time there had been violence, subversion and intimidation by both sides. This included terrorist violence by the IRA and the UVF but it also included street violence and intimidation during the Ulster Workers' Council (UWC) strike in 1974 when Protestant 'loyalists' coerced workers into taking part in an avowedly political strike. Its declared aim was to bring down the only elected government in which power had ever been shared by Protestant and Catholic politicians in proportion to the size of the two communities. Thus the first real hope of reconciliation in

Ireland since 1921 was tragically snuffed out by violent political
action. Stressing that both the IRA and the UWC had used
violence Francis commented:

> Experience of the UWC strike suggests that the BBC's credibility
> depends more on impartiality than balance and our responsi-
> bility lies as much in reflecting the significance of voices of the
> people, including subversion, as in sustaining institutions of
> democracy not wholly accepted.[8]

He went on to say that, if the BBC invariably supported the
government and suppressed the views of all who dissented, it
would lose all influence with those members of the public whose
views mattered most – the uncommitted ones[9] whom the terrorists would hope to recruit as supporters but who might be persuaded instead that life without terrorism would be better. Merely
preaching to the converted would contribute nothing to the resolu-
tion of the conflict.

Robin Walsh, also serving with the BBC in Northern Ireland,
said in a lecture to the Royal United Services Institute:

> The BBC, argue the critics, should support law and order. I
> suggest that it is its duty to *report* law and order. To support it in
> the way that many would have it do would be to turn a blind eye
> to illegalities and would do little for the credibility of the
> security forces. In a nutshell, I think that the BBC has the public
> interest at heart, but surely the public interest is not solving the
> problem and it cannot be solved without being understood by
> the people among whom it exists.[10]

A hard or pompous line achieves nothing. When a Colonel tried to
persuade a *Guardian* reporter not to report an alleged mis-
demeanour by a soldier by saying 'For God's sake we are supporting the Government, aren't you on our side?'[11] the reaction was
predictable.

Perhaps *The Times* put the argument best in a leader about
'The Press, The Army and Ulster'

> . . . The security authorities and the press have essentially dif-
> ferent tasks . . . In conditions of near civil war the army are
> engaged in a conflict that is both military and psychological.
> Because they are fighting urban terrorists who are pursuing

their political ends without scruple or regard for the democratic wishes of the people in either part of Ireland . . . there is an unqualified national interest in the army's success in this struggle. Yet that success cannot be obtained without the sustained support of public opinion, so the security authorities are engaged in a propaganda war which it is in the national interest that they should win.

The press, however, while sharing in the general national interest, have different responsibilities. A newspaper that is realistic will accept that the army must wage a propaganda war but a newspaper that retains its principles will have no part itself in the conduct of that war. Its task is to see that its readers are informed as fully and clearly as possible. That includes not merely the events on the ground but the nature of the conflict, political attitudes on both sides, the relationship of the IRA to the local community and the changing strength of the organisation itself . . .

It would also be a loss if the press were to be inhibited from performing that other part of its function: to provide a check against the use of unjustifiable means in a good cause. Every terrorist organization alleges that its people are tortured. The scrutiny of the press as well as the actions of the authorities have denied the IRA the benefit of that propaganda weapon.[12]

That was how the problem was seen editorially. A great deal of responsibility, however, has fallen upon the individual reporter, not to put lives unnecessarily at risk. Another *Guardian* reporter, Simon Winchester, was watching an angry crowd of Orangemen milling around the Catholic Unity Flats, a well-known flash point. He was aware, though the crowd was not, that a Protestant boy had just been shot in East Belfast.

Naturally enough I kept quiet. But what if I had been working for the BBC and had reported the shooting; and what if one of the Loyalists in that crowd had had a transistor set? I began to have doubts, from that moment on, about the precise role the press – and particularly the broadcasters – were playing in Ireland. Would not this have been the ideal case for some kind of self-censorship, I wondered? Did we always have to report everything we saw, as we saw it, warts and all?[13]

Richard Francis, however, disagrees:

> It's also been suggested that if there is trouble in the town we
> should not report it until it is over. One case quoted was when
> there was a riot going on in West Belfast during the course of
> which four Protestants were shot in East Belfast. It was sug-
> gested that we should have withheld broadcasting that in-
> formation till after the riot in the other part of the town was
> over. I don't accept that at all. In a town like Belfast, which is
> like a village, rumour can travel faster even than radio. If we
> had not announced unequivocally that four Protestants had
> been shot, the rioting crowds would likely have made it not four
> but fourteen, not shot but dead and the riot could have been
> very much worse than it was.[14]

Just as the soldiers and policemen learned that it was in their
interest to retain the goodwill of the media, so editors and journalists learned that they too needed to retain the goodwill of the army
and the RUC. If a reporter proved that he could not be trusted to
honour an off-the-record or non-attributable agreement for a
briefing or discussion, he knew that he would never get another
one. Similarly, if a reporter proved that he had a hostile bias or was
likely to seek information to pass on to the IRA, they would warn
officers and soldiers on the ground not to trust him. He would
therefore become useless and his editor would replace him.

A good investigative reporter will inevitably discover information which, if reported, could put lives at risk. He may then face a
dilemma in that his information reveals improper practices which
it is in the public interest to terminate. In some cases, however, he
has to balance his duty to disclose with his responsibility for consequent risk to life. In such cases he will be sorely tempted to get his
scoop but if lives are hazarded or lost he may prejudice his future
prospects as a reporter. A more advisable and ethical solution
might be to bring the malpractice to the notice of the authorities
rather than to publish it.

An example of this occurred in 1976. Robert Fisk, reporting for
The Times, published a report that army intelligence personnel
were using forged press cards,[15] a practice which was both unethical
and unwise, and placed the lives of *bona fide* journalists at risk. The
Secretary of State forbade the practice immediately – clearly a
success for investigative reporting. There was, nevertheless, a risk

that its publication might enable the IRA to identify plain clothes personnel who had recently used forged press cards which could result at worst in their murder and at best in their being unable to continue their work. Either of these would help the IRA and prejudice the gathering of intelligence — the key factor in protecting the public against them. It is, however, arguable that only if the authorities are publicly punished for unwise or improper practices will they be deterred from committing or permitting others. In all normal circumstances that would be a fair and convincing justification of investigative reporting. When lives are at stake, however, the reporter and editor have to balance their duty as journalists against their duty as citizens not to risk lives by assisting the terrorists or hampering the police or the army.

In this respect, as in others, the terrorists enjoy an advantage in that the investigative reporter can probe the army or police with no risk more serious than forfeiting their co-operation, but if he attempted a similar probe into the terrorist organization he would forfeit his life. The fact that the lawful authorities are subject to scrutiny, which the terrorists evade by terrorizing the journalists, has a healthy effect in underlining their totally different ethical standards — provided that the public is constantly reminded of this difference.

This leads to the question of news black-out requests. This is of general application, especially in cases of kidnapping and other direct threats to lives, so its discussion will be deferred to Chapters 11, 12 and 13.

CONCLUSION

To sum up: the conflict in Northern Ireland has been primarily a propaganda war. Violence has played its part in grabbing the news headlines (armed propaganda) and in provoking overreaction, but whenever the violence has resulted in killing on any large scale, either by the security forces or by the terrorists, it has most often been counter-productive — as on Bloody Sunday and Bloody Friday.

In a deeply divided community, both the Protestant and Catholic extremists developed a hostility towards the security forces and, very often, towards unbiased journalists, each side feeling that their bias was towards its enemy.

The terrorists, being usually the initiators of violent incidents, could usually win the race for the news, being ready with their story in advance. The army and police had to check the facts before they issued their version, and paid a heavy price in credibility if they had to correct it later. Within this constraint, it paid them to report the truth, officially, as quickly as possible, warts and all. Being answerable themselves to the law, they might all too soon be barred from doing so, and from countering terrorist dis-information, if the case became *sub judice*.

The risk of allowing junior NCOs and soldiers to appear on television — direct into the living room — proved fully justified. They provided the best counter to terrorist propaganda. Police constables, however, were inhibited from doing this because of their potential involvement in any prosecution.

Journalists in Northern Ireland, often young ones sent to prove themselves, were subject to exceptional temptations and pressures, lures and threats, from all sides. Some succumbed to these, though most faced them with courage and integrity. They often faced a dilemma of conscience, when their duty to investigate and publish clashed with the risk to lives if they did so.

On balance, the army and police gained from the reporting of the media. By 1978 the number of terrorist murders was cut to a quarter of its 1972 level (bringing the homicide rate in Belfast down to a third of the rate in Washington DC). The contributions from the Irish American community to the IRA were similarly reduced. Both the army and the RUC maintained high levels of recruiting, filling their ranks entirely with volunteers. The great majority of people of both communities in Northern Ireland would still rather have soldiers or policemen in the streets than gunmen of either side.

Above all, Northern Ireland proved that, in dealing with political violence, the television camera is the most powerful weapon available to either side if they can learn how to use it.

11 Access to the Media for Terrorists

INCIDENTS AND INTERVIEWS

There is a fundamental difference between reporting violent incidents and screening television interviews with the terrorists themselves. Terrorists use armed propaganda to seize the attention of the public and the ethics of giving them the publicity they seek by reporting such violent incidents were discussed in the previous chapter. At the same time terrorists or their supporters will seek every opportunity to put their case directly on television in interviews, possibly back-to-camera, and this chapter is concerned with the wisdom, ethics and legality of giving them such opportunities.

Both of these dilemmas were well posed in 1977 by Richard Francis, then Controller of BBC Northern Ireland:

> If the violent activities of terrorists go unreported there must be a danger that they may escalate their actions to make their point. And if we don't seek, with suitable safeguards, to report and to expose the words of terrorist front organizations, we may well be encouraging them to speak more and more with violence.[1]

Three years later, as Director, News and Current Affairs, he wrote:

> I cannot really believe that our society is afraid of the *views* of terrorist gangs. It is their actions with which they speak loudest — the shattered car, the pool of blood, the burnt out home. And the simple fact is that the amount of publicity given to the effects of terrorist action is far and away in excess of the highly selective exercise involved in the occasional programme or

interview which seeks to illuminate the underlying reasons for these acts.[2]

Between 1971 and 1979 there were six BBC television interviews with members of Irish terrorist organizations (IRA, INLA and UVF), and many more with their legal front organizations. In the 12-month period October 1975–6, for example, BBC Northern Ireland Television broadcast six interviews with spokesmen of Provisional Sinn Fein and twelve with spokesmen for the Protestant paramilitaries.[3] The terrorist interviews included two with David O'Connell (Provisional IRA Chief of Staff) in 1971 and 1974, one with UVF leaders in 1975, one with an INLA representative (back to camera) in February 1977, one with a number of Provisional IRA leaders, including MacStiofan, O'Brady and O'Connell,[4] in December 1977 and one with an INLA spokesman on 5 July 1979. All of these provoked outraged comment in the press and usually also in Parliament, the 1979 INLA interview most of all.

THE INLA INTERVIEW, 5 JULY 1979

July 5 1979 was the last programme of *Tonight* which, despite changes of name, had enjoyed a long run as one of the BBC's most popular current affairs programmes. Its editor was Roger Bolton, who was later to be involved as Editor of *Panorama* in the controversy over filming the IRA at Carrickmore (see pages 115–19). The *Tonight* team were understandably determined that their last programme should be one to be remembered.

Since the tenth anniversary of the deployment of British troops in the Province was approaching, it was decided to do a programme about Northern Ireland. A request to the Secretary of State (Humphrey Atkins) to take part was declined. Roger Bolton obtained BBC approval (the BBC procedures for such approval are discussed later in the chapter) to approach the INLA, which had hit the headlines on 30 March 1979 by murdering the Shadow Secretary of State, Airey Neave, MP, within the precincts of Parliament. Up till then, few people had heard of the INLA, a very small movement believed to be less than 50 strong.

At the time the *Tonight* team made its first contact, the INLA had not yet been made illegal. During the intervening week, before the interview was recorded and broadcast, however, the

British Government banned the INLA under the Prevention of Terrorism Act. The matter was again considered by Richard Francis and the Director-General of the BBC and it was decided to broadcast the interview on the grounds that it would help the public to understand the reasons for the ban.[5]

The interviewer, David Lomax, after making the initial contact in Dublin, received a telephone call giving instructions which led to a series of different hotels, in each of which he and his camera team were presumably monitored to ensure that they were not leading or being followed by the police. Eventually they found themselves in a room which had been booked in Lomax's name in a hotel on the outskirts of Dublin. Here they were received by two men wearing wigs, false moustaches and dark glasses and wearing rubber gloves. They had 'strange bulges' in their anorak pockets and Lomax was satisfied that the man interviewed was, as he claimed, a spokesman for the INLA.[6]

The man insisted on being interviewed back to camera. He used the opportunity for a rather turgid 'party political broadcast' for the INLA, despite skilful questioning and control of the interview by David Lomax. His justification for the murder consisted mainly of a Marxist critique of British society and a number of personal attacks on Mr Neave, including a statement that he was an advocate of torture. At that point, during the screening, the recording was interrupted by a studio statement from David Lomax refuting this and some of the other allegations, pointing out that Airey Neave, having suffered at the hands of the Nazis in the notorious Colditz camp was well known for his opposition to torture in any form. This was forcefully confirmed in a discussion later in the same programme by one of his political opponents, Northern Irish Catholic MP Gerry Fitt, who also pointed out that the INLA spokesman revealed by his accent that he was not a Northern but a Southern Irishman.[7]

The BBC did not tell the police in advance about either the recording or the broadcast, though Lomax did warn the INLA spokesman that everything they saw and filmed might later be used in evidence.[8] Though the BBC attempted to avoid advance publicity, Irish Republican newspapers got hold of the story (presumably from the INLA) and ran it on the morning of 5 July, thus giving some 16 hours' notice of the broadcast. The BBC thereafter had some discussion with the Northern Ireland office, and there was intense argument within the BBC during the afternoon before it decided, in what Francis later described as a '55–45 decision', to go ahead. The BBC also notified the Neave family, which they thought better than telephoning Airey Neave's widow direct, but they thought she was unlikely to be watching and unfortunately the message was not passed on to her. She happened to be watching television, alone, when the interview came on, and was naturally both surprised and distressed.

Reaction was at first muted. The estimated audience was about one million and the BBC received only 87 telephone calls – no more than they would expect to get for broadcasting a four-letter word.[9] The following week, however, the *Daily Telegraph* published a letter from Lady Neave, complaining that the programme had 'betrayed the traditional standards of British broadcasting'. This was followed by an editorial calling for new laws to restrain the broadcasting of interviews with terrorists.[10] On the same day the Prime Minister, in reply to a question in Parliament, said that the matter had been referred to the Attorney General, and added: 'I am appalled that it was ever transmitted and I believe it reflects gravely on the judgement of the BBC and those who are responsible for the decision.'[11]

Thereafter controversy raged and, if the interview did nothing else, it aroused a searching re-examination of both the ethics and the laws governing interviews with terrorists. The BBC broadcast a discussion on Sunday 15 July, in *The Editors* series, in which participants included Merlyn Rees, ex Secretary of State for Northern Ireland and Home Secretary at the time of Airey Neave's murder; William Deedes, Editor of the *Daily Telegraph* and a close friend of the Neave family; Richard Francis of the BBC; John Birt, Controller of Current Affairs, London Weekend Television; Roy Lilley, Editor of a Northern Irish newspaper; and Jane Ewart-Biggs, widow of the British Ambassador assassinated by the IRA in Dublin in 1976. A week later (22 July) ITV *State of the Nation* broadcast a 'hypothetical' – a form of discussion developed at the Harvard Law School in which people play their own or similar roles (e.g., a reporter from one newspaper may be asked to deal with the editor of another as if it were his own) in discussing a hypothetical situation. In this case, though the movement was not named and the programme was recorded before the INLA interview, the hypothetical situation was very similar except that the initiative came from the other side in the form of an invitation to meet, in a neighbouring country, a terrorist known to be wanted by the police in both countries. Participants again included Merlyn Rees, Richard Francis and John Birt; also Keith Kyle, a BBC correspondent; Rex Cathcart and Baroness Sharp, both former members of the Independent Broadcasting Authority (IBA); David Nicholas, Editor-in-Chief ITN; Jeremy Wallington, Director of Programmes, Southern Television; David Elstein, an ITV producer; Derek Jameson, Editor of the *Daily Express*, and Chapman Pincher, formerly an *Express* correspondent; Hugo Young of the *Sunday Times*; and Gilbert Kelland, Assistant Commissioner, Scotland Yard.

Some months later in November 1979 the BBC held a two-day hypothetical which was not recorded or broadcast,[12] in which the author took part, this time with a larger number of people, most of whom again held or had held responsible positions as newspaper and television editors and reporters, judges, lawyers, ex-cabinet ministers, MPs, civil servants, senior police and army officers, etc., including representatives of these professions in USA. Although, for obvious reasons, there was no representation of terrorist movements, some of the journalists and others invited had at least some sympathy for them and were known to be highly critical of the government, police and army in Northern Ireland. The hypothetical situations discussed covered a wider area but included one concerning an interview with a terrorist.

In all of these discussions, factual or hypothetical, the arguments for and against such broadcasts, the laws governing them and the procedures, guidelines and ethics used by the BBC, ITV and newspapers, were fully examined. They gave an example of the media at their best in helping the community to understand terrorism, thereby assisting protection against it. They provide a rare and remarkable record of the views and conflicting arguments, most of them presented under the lights of a public debate, by people who have been personally involved in taking the decision to conduct terrorist interviews and to publish or broadcast them. These discussions have formed the main basis for the analysis which follows.

THE ETHICS OF BROADCASTING TERRORIST INTERVIEWS

Should the INLA interview have been broadcast? Richard Francis's

case for doing so was put in the quotation at the beginning of this
chapter — that it will have helped the public understand the
reasons for the violence at a price of publicity for the terrorists
which was negligible compared with the publicity they obtained
from the day-to-day reports of the violence itself. Alternatively, to
quote the Director-General of the BBC: 'We believe that the
public has the common sense and stability to judge very accurately
the character of the people they are seeing. They recognize a
murderous thug for what he is.'[13]

Against this it can be argued that the other kind of 'murderous
thug' who kills for criminal gain or hate or revenge is not given,
and should not be given, the privilege of justifying his crime to a
million people on television. Should a criminal who commits the
same crime for what is his own estimate of political justification
have any greater right?

After the second BBC interview with David O'Connell in 1974,
Timothy Raison, MP, criticized the BBC for giving coverage on the
television screen to 'an enemy avowedly at war with Britain'. Others
said it was equivalent to giving airtime to Hitler or Dr Goebbels in
the Second World War. The Bishop of Crediton thought that the
BBC should have telephoned the police and offered to hand the
man over. The then Director-General, Sir Charles Curran, replied
that if the reporter had disclosed O'Connell's whereabouts to the
police, he would have been an immediate target for the attentions
of the IRA, and he thought it unacceptable that any organization
should require its staff to run such a risk. He added: 'The essential
question is whether BBC reporters ought to be asked to undertake
such interviews. Once that question is answered in the affirmative,
the arrangements for the interview preclude disclosure to the police
by the reporter.'

He went on to say that the person making the decision has to
consider 'whether the undeniable wish of the IRA to make propaganda through such interviews will be outbalanced by the value of
the information which will be brought to the attention of the
British public'.[14]

These arguments were repeated almost precisely to justify the
INLA interview in 1979,[15] but Mrs Ewart-Biggs, whose husband
had been murdered by the IRA, felt that the price the community
was asked to pay for being informed was in this case too high; that
the INLA, which was largely unknown until 30 March, was now
extremely well known and had reinforced its position.[16]

The weight of the evidence seems to be strongly in the direction that, on this occasion at least, the broadcast did more harm than good. The public were informed of something of no particular value in exchange for enormous publicity and encouragement for a tiny but vicious movement. On the other hand, the BBC Audience Research surveyed a sizeable sample after the interview and four-fifths thought it had been right to show it.[17]

Perhaps the most significant comments came from Merlyn Rees as an ex-Northern Ireland and Home Secretary. While accepting the general value of such interviews in the sense that the community had a right to know something about the terrorists so that they could make the right judgements, he criticized the BBC in this instance for agreeing to interview the INLA man back to camera. He felt that both the British and Irish police should have been informed. He also warned that the Provisional IRA would have regarded the broadcast as giving extra status to the INLA in their competition for 'who are the greatest guys in the terrorist scene' and asked 'are they going to outdo each other?'[18] His anxiety proved to be justified by the murder of Earl Mountbatten by the Provisional IRA on 27 August 1979 which, though it probably rebounded against them both in the Republic of Ireland and in the USA, certainly brought them a matching publicity splash. This likelihood of cause and effect cannot be overlooked.

CARRICKMORE

In September 1979, in the wake of the INLA controversy and the murder of Mountbatten, BBC *Panorama* began planning a project on the Provisional IRA, examining its history and its contemporary aims and tactics. Two ex-chiefs of staff of the Provisional IRA, David O'Connell and Sean MacStiofan, were to be among those interviewed and their names, along with the outline of the project, were cleared by the Director, News and Current Affairs.[19]

On 17 October Jeremy Paxman, with the production team, were in Dublin where they had already interviewed David O'Connell. They received an anonymous telephone call at their hotel, saying that they would see something interesting if they went to Carrickmore 22 miles north of the border. Whether or not O'Connell had put them up to it, the IRA presumably realized that the BBC team, doing a programme on the IRA, were almost sure to rise to the bait — as they did.

On reaching Carrickmore, a one-street village, the team drove through to the far end without seeing anything and began to drive back. At this point, in the words of Paul Barriff, the cameraman, 'All of a sudden, two men in hoods and carrying guns appeared about 50 yards away and started to walk away from us. I reached for my camera and started filming.'[20]

The nature and quality of the film bear out the team's insistence that it was not pre-planned. On the sound track they can be heard muttering 'shall we get out',[21] but they decided to stay and followed the IRA men to a crossroads where they were joined by five other armed men in balaclavas and they stopped four or five cars, checking their driving licences. The BBC team filmed for about 11 minutes, using 500 feet of film. They then drove on to Belfast and went to bed.

Next day (18 October) they informed the *Panorama* office in London and the Northern Ireland Office. Humphrey Atkins, Northern Ireland Secretary, was also informed on that day and told the Home Secretary, William Whitelaw, soon afterwards. The *Panorama* team also telephoned the BBC lawyers who told them that if they could not recognize any of the men they were not obliged to inform the police.

They did not inform the police or the army directly but when they telephoned the Lisburn press office the next day to confirm a prearranged interview they were told that the army had withdrawn its agreement to co-operate with *Panorama* on the programme.

The BBC's Head of Programmes and Head of News in Belfast were also told by *Panorama* about the film but the BBC Controller Northern Ireland, James Hawthorne, was not informed and the first he heard of it was on 25 October, when he was asked about it at dinner by a senior Northern Ireland Office official.[22]

The BBC programme was due to be screened on 19 November and the decision whether or not to do so was precipitated by the story being reported in the Dublin republican magazine *Hibernia*, whose Belfast-based reporter Ed Maloney had been to Carrickmore to investigate another story. Hearing about the BBC filming in the village and of the army's subsequent attempts to 'close the stable door', he wrote an article, quietly laughing at the discomfiture of the army, the Northern Ireland Office and the British intelligence services. *Hibernia* published the article on 8 November. Knowing in advance (presumably from their supporters in the village) that the story was 'blown', the IRA put out their own version, which was in the hands of the press on the same day:

> In an audacious show of strength, a heavily armed IRA force effectively sealed off the County Tyrone village of Carrickmore and held it for a full three hours while being filmed by a BBC television crew. What is termed as 'undoubtedly one of the IRA's more spectacular propaganda coups to date' happened on the afternoon of October 17th . . .
>
> The whole operation was kept strictly secret even when it was all over. It was only when a reporter from the Dublin magazine *Hibernia* came on the story that the incident leaked out . . .
>
> With the story 'blown' sources involved in the event confirmed the scale of the operation . . . Two M60 machine guns, RPG7 rocket propelled grenade launchers and many Armalite rifles were brought into the village of 400 people for display in front of the cameras.
>
> Defensive positions were set up in the village and the main body of men drilled in the main street. Villagers were filmed chatting to the armed men and going about their business with bizarre scenes continuing around them.
>
> The IRA stayed in control of Carrickmore for three hours in broad daylight and pulled out after the *Panorama* film crew said they had enough footage. The IRA even offered to hold Carrickmore, 22 miles from the border, overnight if necessary . . . Some sources estimate the total size of the force to be in excess of 100 . . .[23]

Certain British and foreign newspapers swallowed the IRA's version in full, largely ignoring the *Hibernia* estimate of 'an IRA patrol understood to have been between 12 and 15 strong'. Many, in fact, exaggerated it still further, speaking of 140 men. Some also printed the BBC's denial, saying that there were at most 10 men, with no machine guns or rocket launchers or drilling in the main square. The BBC admitted, however, that the incident 'would appear to be a clear breach of standing instructions in relation to filming in Ireland'.[24]

Meanwhile, also on 8 November, there was a storm in the House of Commons when the matter was raised in a question to the

Prime Minister. The BBC was accused of 'arranging for IRA gunmen to take over an Ulster village for an afternoon as a stunt', and of
'treasonable activity'. Mrs Thatcher commented that it was not the
first time the government had occasion to raise similar matters with
the BBC and that it was time the BBC 'put its house in order'. The
Leader of the Opposition, James Callaghan, said that it was
distasteful and reprehensible to manufacture news adding: 'It is not
the duty of the media to stage manage news, but to report it.'[25]

Ed Maloney of *Hibernia* was appalled at the gullibility of some
of his colleagues in accepting the IRA's version. He said that half
the things reported were not in his report. There was no parade,
fewer weapons, only one road block and nothing like the 140 IRA
men. He added: 'I'm a full-time journalist. For the first time I'm
really getting an insight into how awful they can be.'[26]

On 13 November, Scotland Yard officers went to the BBC's
Lime Grove studios with a search warrant and seized the film
under the provisions of the Prevention of Terrorism Act.[27]

The BBC had by then decided not to show the film. The Editor
of *Panorama*, Roger Bolton, was subjected to a disciplinary
hearing on the ground that the failure to inform the Controller
Northern Ireland had been in breach of standing instructions. It
was rumoured that he was to be permanently removed to another
post but the staff of *Panorama* gave notice that if he were they
would all walk out. He remained in post, though both he and the
Head of Current Affairs, John Gau, were reprimanded.[28]

The decision not to show the film was a correct one because,
even if the BBC had introduced it by describing the background
and making it clear that it was a performance acted specially for
the cameras, it would still have been wrong for a national broadcasting medium, and especially a public service one, to be seen
publicly not only co-operating with a criminal organization but
also aiding and abetting what they knew to be false propaganda
(the implication that they operated an alternative 'police force' in
areas of their choice at will). The reporter, producer, director and
team were in no way at fault in filming what they saw. They were,
and should be, eager to get news and would be dismal journalists if
they did not find joy in a scoop. While technically they should have
asked permission in advance before filming, they did not know in
advance what they were going to film. When they saw the IRA
men they were fully justified in using their camera, if for no other
reason than that the film might be of use to the police. (The issue

would not be so clear with an electronic news gathering (ENG) camera and this problem will be discussed in Chapter 13.) They did inform their editors but they can be criticized for failing to do this until the next day. They should also have informed the police as soon as they safely could, probably from the first telephone box on the road to Belfast. It was suggested that there might be a *prima facie* case against them under the Prevention of Terrorism Act (1976) which, as Richard Francis himself recognized, 'places a positive onus on persons who have information which might be of material assistance in apprehending anyone involved in an act of terrorism connected with Northern Ireland to disclose it as soon as is reasonably practical'.[29] After consideration of the case, however, the Attorney General announced in the House of Commons in July 1980 that he had decided not to institute criminal proceedings against any BBC staff for either the INLA or the Carrickmore incidents.

The Editors and the higher ranks of the BBC (here it must be recorded that the Director-General, Ian Trethowan, was in hospital throughout this incident and took no part in the decisions) did, however, face some criticism. They should have decided at once not to use the film for the reasons given above (false propaganda by a criminal and illegal organization). Then when the IRA story broke on the world alongside the *Hibernia* version, it could have been dismissed as false without any fuss.

The real offenders were the journalists and editors who swallowed the IRA's story and the politicians who so gullibly overreacted to it. The newspaper editors should at least have checked the story with the BBC, particularly as the republican *Hibernia* had already printed its much more sober version. And the politicians, some of whom had in fact known about the film for several weeks, should have appreciated that their public outbursts of indignation gave the whole story more publicity and the IRA more of a morale booster and more prestige than even the showing of the film would have done. The *Economist* summed it up well: 'Mr. James Callaghan, the Labour leader, was no slower than Mrs. Thatcher to place heavy blame on the BBC for stage-managing the news. Might he — and she — not better have asked whether the IRA was not, there and then, stage-managing Parliament?'[30]

LAWS AND GUIDELINES

In the Republic of Ireland, section 31 of the Broadcasting Authority

Act bars the broadcast of any material calculated to further the aims or objectives of an illegal organization. The British Prevention of Terrorism Act (Temporary Provisions) Act 1976, renewed in 1979, makes it an offence (section 11) for a person to fail to disclose information which he knows or believes might be of material assistance in preventing an act of terrorism or in securing the apprehension, prosecution or conviction of any person for a terrorist offence; it is also an offence (section 1) to arrange a meeting of three or more persons knowing that the meeting is to support or to further the activities of a proscribed organization or is to be addressed by a person belonging or professing to belong to it; or (section 9) knowingly to harbour any person who he knows or believes would be excluded or removed from Great Britain or Northern Ireland under the Act.[31] The journalists involved in the INLA interview and the Carrickmore film might well have been charged under one or more of these provisions, and the BBC senior management involved in the decision to record and broadcast the INLA interview might also have been liable under certain sections of the Act. The fact that the interview took place in the Republic would not remove the onus on anyone subject to British law to pass on the information at once to the British authorities, especially as the person interviewed openly admitted being involved in committing a terrorist crime in Great Britain ('. . . *we* have murdered Airey Neave . . .').

If the interview had been broadcast on RTE (Irish Television) in the Republic they would have been breaking Irish law but, even though a very large number of people in the Republic watch material broadcast from transmitters in UK, the BBC was clearly not subject to the Irish Broadcasting Authority Act.

If a journalist in the UK receives an invitation or himself takes the initiative in arranging to interview a known murderer (political or otherwise) or spokesman for an illegal organization, is he legally obliged to notify the police *before* the interview? If that information is likely to lead to the apprehension of a terrorist then presumably, under the Prevention of Terrorism Act, he is legally so obliged. Some would say that he is also morally obliged by his duty to the public as potential terrorist victims.

These questions were posed and fully explored in the ITV *State of the Nation* discussion described on pages 112–13. Nine editors and reporters from newspapers, BBC and ITV expressed views in the discussion. One experienced reporter said that he would secretly consult friends in the security service (not the police) to see if they could find a mutually acceptable way of gaining intelligence dividends, but that he would not tell his editor that he had done so. The other eight were vehement that they would in no circumstances tell either the security service or the police. They variously argued that this would be a breach of journalistic ethics, would betray the confidence of a source, would ensure that they would never have such opportunities again and would imperil their own lives.[32] Since none of those involved in the INLA interview have been prosecuted it must be presumed that the Director of Public Prosecutions accepted their point of view.

If the law does not in practice prevent such interviews, how do the media's own internal procedures control the ethics of it, and what powers does the government have to intervene?

The BBC's own guidelines require any decision to interview a terrorist in the UK to be referred up the management chain to the Director-General for prior approval. He may discuss the decision with his Board of Management (which includes the Managing Directors of Television and Radio and the Director, News and Current Affairs, amongst others). This clearly seems to have been done in reaching the '55—45' decision to go ahead with the INLA interview. The Director-General accepted responsibility for the decision. The BBC Board of Governors were not involved. All of them, including the Chairman, are part-time and take no part in editorial or operating decisions but they do have the ultimate sanction of hiring or firing the Director-General; they are also responsible for the standards maintained by the BBC, though to ensure editorial freedom for the Board of Management this responsibility is discharged retrospectively as regards individual programmes. Nevertheless, because the Chairman receives the first blast of any ministerial criticism, the Director-General would normally warn him in advance of any programme likely to be controversial.

The IBA plays a more active part in planning programmes. The Television Act requires that nothing should be broadcast which is conducive to the promotion of crime, and the IBA are responsible for implementing the Act. Under the IBA guidelines, the programme companies are required to obtain approval *before* broadcasting a programme if there is any doubt about whether it breaches the Television Act, and such doubts would certainly apply to an interview with a terrorist.

The government does still retain the power, left over from the Second World War, to ban any BBC programme if it thinks fit, but this power has never been used and is unlikely to be used, so long as there is not a right- or left-wing government bent upon control of the media (whether directly or through the guise of committees or a union closed shop for editors). The only externally applied bans so far have been by strikes or threats of strikes called by a union, usually one which controls some small but vital link in the chain, and which objects to material planned for broadcast, but this has been very rare.

There are, however, other deterrents or fears which may lead the BBC Board of Management or the IBA to decide not to make or broadcast a programme. These include the normal laws governing crime, defamation, obscenity, prevention of terrorism, incitement to violence, etc., to which the BBC are as answerable as any other organization. These laws can only be applied by the police (by arrest or seizure) or by the judiciary (retrospectively or by granting an injunction). The government can ask Parliament to change the laws, if necessary by Emergency Legislation (the Prevention of Terrorism Act went through all stages in a week) but normally only after some weeks or months of public debate.

The government does, however, have a more subtle power in the control by Parliament of the BBC's licence fee − of its size and also of its duration. To maintain its editorial freedom the BBC would like the licence fee to be passed by Parliament (with, presumably, an agreed rising scale for inflation) for some years ahead but politicians of both parties prefer annual reconsideration. Despite claims that the reasons are purely economic and social, it is hard to believe that they do not also welcome the leverage this gives them over the BBC Board of Management which they can use, not so much to coerce them into cancelling individual programmes as to maintain a constant deterrent against the BBC doing anything to displease them. This is potentially an ugly form of hidden persuasion which Parliament would do well to end. If powers are needed by government they should be open and direct.

In practice, persuasion is generally (and probably best) applied by informal and confidential discussion between ministers or officials, on the one hand, and Board Members or Editors on the other. An example of such discussion (between the Commissioner of Police and editors) is given in the next chapter. This does, however, require the minister or official knowing that there is a problem to be discussed and he may not be aware of this unless the Board Member or Editor has reported or referred it. He, being human, may be like the small boy who is asked by his mother why he didn't ask her before helping himself to goodies from the larder and says 'Because you would have said no.'

It would be wrong, however tempting, for governments to *require* that the BBC or IBA must refer controversial programmes in advance to the government because that would be *de facto* editorial control by the government and so a sacrifice of the most fundamental of the bulwarks of democracy. If the programme is likely to be in breach of the law, the BBC or ITV legal advisers will warn their Boards who would then proceed only at their own risk. If, however, the breach is of morality, ethics or duty to the community, then the ball comes back into the court of the journalistic profession itself. Whether, like doctors and lawyers, journalists should have their own self-enforced powers of discipline is a question discussed later in this book.

12 Kidnapping

KIDNAP HIDEOUT AND SIEGE SITUATIONS

A kidnap hideout and a siege situation are very different things. In the former, the kidnapped hostages are held in a secret place and their family or friends have to negotiate for their release through intermediaries or anonymous messages or telephone calls without knowing who they are talking to or where the victims are. The police are involved only indirectly in these negotiations. In a siege situation, however, where both the kidnappers and their hostages are surrounded in a known location, it is the police who handle the negotiations.

A siege can develop from a hideout situation if the police discover where the hideout is, as occurred when the IRA kidnapped Dr Tiede Herrema in the Republic of Ireland in 1975. More often, however, a siege situation begins when terrorists seize a building and hold its occupants at gunpoint, threatening to kill them unless their political demands are met or unless they are guaranteed safe conduct to another country. An example of this was the seizure of the Iranian Embassy in London on 30 April 1980. Siege situations may also begin when a group of terrorists or criminals are cornered by the police in a building and sieze hostages in the hope of bargaining for their own release or, possibly, giving time for accomplices elsewhere to flee to safety. An example of this was the Balcombe Street siege in London in 1975.

There are variants: a hijacked aircraft in the air is hardly besieged, though it becomes so as soon as it lands; and on at least one occasion (see the case of Alio Kaloghirou below) the police did discover the location of the secret hideout but judged it better not to let the kidnappers know that they knew, nor to mount an overt siege.

Hostage-taking of all kinds reached an unprecedented level in the 1970s. During the decade there were over 1000 reported cases in police records and, since many cases are settled for a ransom without the victim's family ever telling the police, the actual number was probably several thousand. Of these, the majority were by criminals for criminal gain but at least 400 were by political terrorists [1] to exert political blackmail, to get publicity or to extort funds for their political movement. The largest number of criminal kidnappings was in Europe (mainly Italy) and the majority of political kidnappings were in Latin America. In 1979—80, there was a sharp rise in raids on embassies and seizures of diplomatic hostages.

The media play a crucial role in both hideout and siege situations. Positively, they can be a channel, sometimes the only channel, whereby information can be fed to the kidnappers, either as part of the negotiating process or as a psychological or tactical ploy. Negatively, irresponsibility or thoughtlessness by the media can gravely prejudice the chances of successful negotiation or rescue of the hostages. The examples considered in this chapter will be those in which the victim was taken to a secret hideout. Siege situations will be examined in the next chapter.

PETER LORENZ AND HANNS-MARTIN SCHLEYER

Sometimes the media have — or feel that they have — little option but to dance to the terrorists' tune. In February 1975 German terrorists kidnapped Peter Lorenz, Christian Democrat candidate for Mayor of West Berlin, just before the election, demanding the release of six of their convicted comrades from prison. Though the Federal Government in Bonn was involved in the release of the prisoners, West Berlin is largely autonomous so the incumbent Social Democrat Mayor played a leading role in the decisions. This placed him under tremendous pressures as he was reluctant to take a hard line when his opponent's life was at stake. After three days the government gave in. One of the six whose release was demanded, Horst Mahler, chose to remain in prison pending the end of his sentence in Germany but the other five were flown to Aden with 20 000 DM each.[2] Meanwhile, as one TV editor told Melvin Lasky, of *Encounter* magazine, the event took possession of the television screens:

We just lost control of the medium. It was theirs . . . not ours
. . . We shifted shows in order to meet their timetable . . . There

is plenty of underworld crime on our screens, but up until now
Kojak and Columbo were always in charge . . . Now it was the
real thing, and it was the gangsters who wrote the script and
programmed the mass media. We preferred to think that we
were being 'flexible' but actually we were just helpless, as
helpless as the police and the Bonn Government.[3]

Both the German Government and the German media, however, learned from this experience (Lorenz was their first political
hostage) and worked together admirably when Dr Hanns-Martin
Schleyer was kidnapped in Cologne in September 1977. The
editors knew early on that the German Government was going to
make no concessions (Schleyer himself had left letters to this effect
and, with lone and silent heroism, never wavered throughout his
ordeal). The press, however, kept this secret because, had the
kidnappers known, they would have killed Schleyer at once, since
their only remaining dividend from his body would be to prove the
credibility of their threats. The German Government also skilfully
encouraged the terrorists in the belief that, despite their public
insistence on no concessions, they might in fact be ready to give
way. Ministers and senior officials flew on unspecified missions to
such likely terrorist havens as Aden and Algiers, where they took
care to be spotted by journalists. The consequent conjecture in the
world press again encouraged the kidnappers to keep Schleyer
alive. In fact, they did not kill him for six weeks, when the failure
of the linked hijack operation at Mogadishu and the consequent
suicide in prison of the comrades whose release they were demanding made it pointless to keep him alive any longer. During those six
weeks the German police twice narrowly missed rescuing him, in
each case locating the hideout a day or two too late. Their failure,
due once to bad luck and once to bad management, should not be
allowed to obscure the model of excellent government-media
handling of the case in the joint interest of saving the hostage's life
and arresting the kidnappers.[4]

THE BRITISH EXPERIENCE

The British authorities and the British media also had to go
through their own learning curve. The kidnapping (by a pair of
criminals, not political terrorists) of Mrs Muriel McKay in 1969

was the first major kidnapping[5] for ransom in Britain for many years. The kidnappers (who had incidentally got the wrong victim) telephoned their ransom demand direct to Scotland Yard. The subsequent police investigation was conducted in a glare of publicity. Telephone lines were blocked, and detectives and relatives were relentlessly followed by journalists. Sir Robert Mark considered that this almost certainly ensured the death of the victim[6] – even though it did not prevent the kidnappers later being caught and convicted of murder.

The next major kidnapping in Britain was also mishandled, this time by the police, but is of interest in that there was an attempt, in the event fruitless and misguided, to 'use' the media to mislead the kidnappers. A 17-year-old girl, Lesley Whittle, was kidnapped in January 1975 by a lone criminal, Donald Nielson. Her brother Ronald obeyed instructions to take the ransom money to a telephone box some 60 miles from his home. He had, despite warnings not to do so, informed the police who placed the area under heavy surveillance. Unfortunately, due to lack of co-ordination, the police presence was blown and Nielson never appeared. Thereafter for several weeks Ronald Whittle and the police officer in charge of the case conducted an elaborate charade on television, appearing separately, to try to give the impression that, while they had been in contact, they had now fallen out and that Ronald was negotiating behind their backs. In the event there was no further contact, and seven weeks later Lesley's body was found, hanged, in a drainage shaft close to the rendezvous – almost certainly killed when Nielson took fright at the first bungled attempt to monitor the ransom handover. Nielson was eventually convicted but, once again, without saving the life of the victim.

These two failures no doubt influenced both the police and the media in the successful handling of three other incidents, all in London, during the closing months of 1975. Two of these were sieges – at Spaghetti House and Balcombe Street, and the latter will be briefly described in the next chapter. The third was a hideout kidnap of a 17-year-old Cypriot girl, Alio Kaloghirou, in November 1975. Her kidnappers, as is usual, warned her family not to tell the police but they did. Fortunately they had at that stage told no one else at all so the police were able to tap the telephone and monitor the entire negotiating process without the kidnappers ever suspecting it. The police managed to locate the hideout but they decided that, rather than raid it, they would do better to watch it, disguised as delivery men, road workers, etc., while negotiations were continued, in apparent secrecy, by the family.

To achieve this it was vital that the press should not leak the story, even accidentally. The Commissioner of the Metropolitan Police, Sir Robert Mark, therefore invited the editors of all national newspapers and of BBC News and ITN for a briefing at Scotland Yard, where he told them the story and begged them not to hazard the girl's life by reporting anything about it. He promised to brief their representatives every day, and to tell them all, simultaneously, when the story could be told.

Presented with such a request most newsmen would respect it as a matter of conscience. In case there had been any unable to resist the temptation, however, Sir Robert had effectively deterred them by his shrewd decision to brief them all together. This made them all confident that the others were not stealing a march on them; they also knew that, if anyone did, and the girl were killed, he would be crucified by the others. The strategem succeeded. The press maintained a total black-out. After eleven days the ransom was paid, the girl released, the kidnappers arrested, the money recovered and the story published.

There had, in fact, been two less widely-known precedents for Sir Robert's action 18 years earlier in Malaya where the Emergency was in its closing stages and, though the country was independent with a Malayan Prime Minister, there were still at his request British officers acting as his Director of Operations, Commissioner of Police and Director of Special Branch.

In October 1957 a senior Political Commissar from the Communist guerrilla organization in Perak gave himself up to the police and six months later Hor Lung, the guerrilla commander for the whole of South Malaya, surrendered in Johore. In neither case did their fellow guerrillas know that they had defected and in each case a British Special Branch officer with the Malayan police persuaded them (with the prospect of large rewards) to go back regularly into the jungle, in guerrilla uniform, to persuade others to surrender or, should they not be minded to do so, to enable the police or the army to locate and capture them. They did this, at ever-increasing personal risk, for respectively six months and four months, unsuspected by their comrades, until every surviving guerrilla in their entire commands − 118 in Central Perak and 160 in Johore − was in the hands of the police.

The Prime Minister, Tunku Abdul Rahman realized the potential of these operations, in view of the prestige and authority of the Commissar and Hor Lung in the guerrilla movement. He knew that their success, and the survival of the two key defectors depended utterly on secrecy. He also knew that, since it would take a long time, someone in the press was bound to run across some kind of clue. He therefore called together all the editors of newspapers, radio and press agencies, and took them fully into his confidence, convincing them of the need for secrecy. His task was made easier by the Emergency Regulations in force at the time but it was, nevertheless, a remarkable achievement, both by the Tunku and by the editors. The guerrillas never recovered from the shock of discovering, when the story broke, that their entire organization in South Malaya and Central Perak had stolen away, gang by gang, while their leaders were ostensibly still going about their duties in the jungle. Thereafter, the collapse of the rest of their organization was swift, and by 1960 the Malayan people were rid of the war — and of the Emergency Regulations — which had plagued them for the past twelve years.[7]

THE SCHILD FAMILY

Another story that ended happily was that of the Schild family in 1979–80, though in this case the media began by showing appalling irresponsibility, only partly redeemed by an impressive demonstration of discretion at the end.

Rolf Schild was a British businessman who had a vacation villa in Sardinia. In the early hours of Tuesday, 21 August 1979, he and his wife and 15-year-old daughter Annabel were kidnapped by bandits on their way back to their villa from dinner with friends. Initially there was some mystery and conjecture about their disappearance, because it was over two weeks before any ransom demand was published or indeed before it was known for sure that they had been kidnapped, This conjecture arose because Mr Schild was known to be facing a writ from a merchant bank claiming £3 million which he was alleged to owe them, arising from an earlier business deal.[8] Press conjecture about this was unfortunate, though not surprising, in view of the disappearances of other businessmen in similar circumstances.

Where the media did show inexcusable irresponsibility, however, was in its public and detailed assessment of the size of ransom he might be able to pay. A few days after the kidnap, British newspapers were vying with each other to produce breakdowns of the value of his assets and some specifically reported that he had sold a business he had founded for £2.75 million. Later, in a BBC television programme, a newspaper City correspondent was invited to give — and gave — a detailed valuation of Mr Schild's share holdings and an estimate of how much he could raise if his houses in England and Sardinia were sold. The programme was broadcast live, so even if the producer or interviewer had had doubts about the wisdom of this information going out (though there was no sign that they did) they could not have cut it except by pulling the plug on the transmission. It is fair to add that, by that time, there had already been so much media discussion of Mr Schild's finances that most of the damage was already done, though the BBC — by virtue of its authority and of its instant reach to the ends of the earth — should not have added to it. This example does, however, underline the danger of live broadcasts on sensitive subjects when lives are at stake.[9]

The effect of all this media discussion was disastrous and almost certainly added to the length of the ordeal which the family had to suffer (213 days). It became clear to Mr Schild at the start that the kidnappers intended to negotiate the ransom with him direct. He knew (as most businessmen in Italy know) the normal pattern and scale of such negotiations in Italy. The kidnappers usually started with a demand of the order of £500 000 to £1 million which would be a good deal more than they expected to get. It was rare for this process to take more than five or six weeks and Mr Schild expected that he would eventually have to settle for about £200 000.

For the first few days, though discussion of the ransom was inhibited by lack of an interpreter, the kidnappers remained calm. On the fourth or fifth day, however, they came in great excitement and showed him local papers in which, although he could not read Italian, he could see the big headlines, the names of companies with which he had been involved and the figures £2 million and £2.75 million quoted from British newspapers.

It is customary for the Italian media not to publish fact or conjecture about the wealth of kidnap victims or their families. They have learned this after 70 or 80 kidnaps a year in Italy (there were seven other kidnapped hostages already held in Sardinia alone at the time of the Schild kidnap[10]), since both editors and their readers realize that such publication would reduce the chances of their safe release. When, however, the British media indulged in apparently unbridled investigation and publication of their estimates of the Schilds' wealth the Italian press felt themselves to be released from their normal self-imposed restraint.

The effect was predictable. The ecstatic bandits flourished the papers, saying 'You didn't tell us, did you, how rich you were!'[11] A few days later they separated him from his family and said that it would be bad for them unless he paid what they were asking — twenty milliard lire, which is £11 million. During the following week he did manage to persuade them that this was out of the question, and they reduced it to five milliard (just under £3 million — presumably based on the £2.75 million about which they had read in the press). He said that the most he could raise would be a little over half a milliard (about £380 000). They laughed in his face and reminded him again that they knew how rich he was. They then set him loose on 5 September (after two weeks in captivity) without seeing his family again and with dire warnings of what would happen to them if he failed to raise the money. He returned to England and a long and exhausting process of negotiation through various intermediaries began. After two months the demand was reduced to £1 million, but was raised again to £3 million after the bandits had angrily torn up an advance 'on account' of 20 million lire (£11 000) delivered by an intermediary.

In December, the Italian police made a number of arrests and it looked as though the remaining bandits might be more ready to settle, but early in January Mr Schild complained that negotiations were being hampered by 'fantasies and falsehoods' in the media. 'If all the journalists would leave Sardinia', he said, 'there might be a chance for negotiations to succeed and ensure the safe release of my wife and daughter.' He added that press conjectures, badly translated and heard by the bandits on Italian radio, presented a terrible danger and that the bandits might consider a large number of journalists just as threatening as the police.[12]

On 14 January he paid a ransom of £350 000 but only his wife was released and Annabel was kept in captivity for another two months. She was relatively well treated, having become something of a favourite with her kidnappers, but the family was intensely anxious and appealed to the media not to reveal the news that Mrs Schild had been released. To their credit, this request was respected for two months, though a large number of editors and journalists all over the world must have been aware of the secret.

Eventually, with the Schilds' agreement, the silence was dramatically broken by the Pope on 16 March. He made a moving appeal to the kidnappers to release Annabel in a public address in St Peter's Square, which was filmed and broadcast widely on television and radio. At the same time, intermediaries carried messages from the bandits already arrested and awaiting trial, saying that they would receive relatively light sentences if Annabel were released, but maximum sentences if any harm came to her. Under this double pressure, and fearful that the police were closing in, the bandits cut their losses and released Annabel without further ransom on 22 March — six days after the Pope's appeal.

Though they made some restitution by their universal two months black-out of the news of Mrs Schild's release, the media had unforgivably hampered the process of securing the release of the family from the start. But for the irresponsibility of the British media, it is likely that the family's ordeal would have been over in a few weeks instead of seven months. Mrs Schild and Annabel both survived their captivity with remarkable strength and courage, which so impressed their kidnappers that it probably saved them from mutilation or death. Nevertheless, the sum of human anguish which these seven months involved for everyone concerned was immeasurable.

The media's guidelines and response to requests for news black-outs are discussed at the end of the next chapter. In this case, however, most of the damage was done before there was anyone in a position to request a black-out. The journalists concerned should have had the common sense and imagination to impose their own restraint. This was another case of reckless use of the power of the media in such a way as to put lives at risk. It is to the eternal disgrace of the British media that they compared so badly with the Italian press in this respect — but the Italians had learned the hard way.

13   Siege and Rescue

A HONEY POT FOR JOURNALISTS

A siege situation can seldom be kept secret. This was no doubt one of the reasons why the police in the Alio Kaloghirou case, even though they had discovered the hideout, decided not to besiege it. The blocking of streets, if nothing else, will attract attention and the surrounded house will quickly become a honey pot for journalists. The police have to live with this and steer a course between attempting a total barricade of the area or being so lax that the media, wittingly or unwittingly, destroy the chances of a successful rescue. They have to accept the fact that some journalists will go to any lengths to get news and that controlled co-operation may in the end yield better results.

Captain Frank Bolz, of the New York Police Hostage Squad, has vividly described an example of these difficulties. His policemen, besieging a house where criminals were holding hostages, closed the street and cleared the area of reporters in order to creep up on the house and rescue the hostages. The staff of a local radio station, however, were determined to scoop the story. They got a street directory and telephoned each house in the vicinity until they found someone who could see the scene from his window.

'You can see the hostage house?'

'Yes — I'm looking at it right now.'

'OK, brother you're on the air. Tell the listeners what you can see.'

'Well, there's a group of policemen working along the street. They're hiding in a doorway just two doors down. Then there's a couple more climbing along the roof. There's a skylight up there. It must be in the attic of the hostage house and I think they're making for that.'[1]

Accepting the likelihood of the kidnappers having a radio, the action of the radio station in broadcasting this interview live can again only be described as wilfully or recklessly putting innocent

lives at risk, in knowing defiance of the wishes of the police attempting to save the hostages. There was a similar, though less flagrant,
defiance by a cameraman at the London Iranian Embassy siege in
1980, though his editors took more care to reduce the risk of
endangering the operation. This example will be examined more
fully later, but both cases raise the question of whether there should
be legal or other restraints to deter such actions, and this question
will be further explored later in the book.

By contrast, the media behaved with commendable responsibility at the Spaghetti House and Balcombe Street sieges in
London in 1975. An important factor in this was that Sir Robert
Mark, then Commissioner of the Metropolitan Police, personally
briefed the press on a number of occasions, told them all he could,
and explained how they could best avoid hazarding the hostages'
lives. At the end of the Balcombe Street siege he used the media
positively by deliberately leaking the news that the Special Air
Service (SAS) soldiers were standing by to launch an assault.
Though this was four and a half years before their raid on the
Iranian Embassy, the reputation of the SAS was already such that
the IRA kidnappers decided to surrender without delay.

THE SIEGE OF THE IRANIAN EMBASSY IN LONDON

The Metropolitan Police, with the attitudes and procedures
developed by Sir Robert Mark and practised at Balcombe Street,
had the machinery to co-operate with the media when six terrorists
broke into the Iranian Embassy at Prince's Gate in London on 30
April 1980. The six came from the Iraqi backed Arab minority in
the Iranian Province of Khuzestan. Twenty-six hostages were
seized, including a policeman (Trevor Lock) and two BBC men
(Sim Harris and Chris Cramer). In response to a 'panic button'
alarm signal from PC Lock, the first police squad was on the scene
within three minutes, and the Metropolitan Police organization
for handling the press went into operation at once, in parallel with
the standard procedures for containment, establishment of communication and negotiation.

They wisely allocated specific and controlled vantage points to
the main cameras which flooded the scene from the world's newspapers and television networks. Had they not done so, it is beyond
doubt that many more of them would have occupied illicit and

uncontrolled vantage points in neighbouring windows[2] – as some of them did.

The police periodically briefed the press, sometimes on the record and sometimes confidentially, usually giving reasons for requests not to report or photograph any particular place or occurrence. Generally these requests were complied with, but not always. The police asked, for example, that the terrorists' first deadline (noon on 1 May), should not be published several hours after it had been telephoned direct to the BBC and broadcast, so most papers repeated it.

Coverage, including live television coverage, was full and continuous throughout the six-day siege. On a number of occasions the police specifically asked the media to report or broadcast certain information (though never false information) because they hoped that this would be heard by the kidnappers and would have a desired psychological effect on them. The BBC insisted that they could not broadcast directed messages as such, but did in fact broadcast them because they were invariably of news value in themselves. For the most part the journalists concerned behaved impeccably, knowing that lives were at stake and also having much to gain from retaining police goodwill. The BBC, for example, agreed to make one of Sim Harris's line managers, Tony Crabb, available to assist the police negotiators by joining them outside the embassy windows to receive directly a request from the terrorists to broadcast certain information. Crabb made it clear, however, that the BBC could not agree to broadcast a dictated message of any kind but merely to include suitable material, edited like any other news, in their normal reports. The terrorists accepted this.

As in the Lorenz kidnapping in Berlin, however, the media at Prince's Gate were in a sense hijacked by the terrorists. This was also the term used by Professor John Gunn who was psychiatric adviser to the police negotiators throughout the siege.[3] The terrorists chose London as the site for their 'television spectacular' because they believed its media coverage to be the best in the world; also because, with its large number of Arab and other Islamic residents and visitors, London has one of the largest concentrations of Arabic journals in the world, representing every shade of opinion from conservative Saudi to radical Libyan and Iraqi. London has been described as 'The information capital of the Middle East'.[4] It is no surprise that, amongst the 26 hostages, no less than five worked in the media, three of them on Middle Eastern journals. They all happened to be in the embassy at the time on various business.

The terrorists' primary aim — indeed probably the only aim they actually hoped to achieve — was to draw attention to their cause. They cannot have seriously expected the Iranian Government to give way to their initial demand to release 91 prisoners from gaols in Iran; this demand and their various deadlines, which they allowed to pass virtually without comment, were simply a basis on which to stage the performance, which they knew would capture the world's headlines. There was a close parallel with the South Moluccan train hijacks in the Netherlands — before which few people in the world had ever heard of the South Moluccan Islands. Before April 1980 few people knew of the existence of an Arab minority in Iran. Now all the world has heard of it.

Professor Gunn also criticized the media (though they hotly contest this) for recklessness in broadcasting reports, in some cases inaccurate ones, without first checking them with the police, both for their accuracy and to ensure that they would not endanger the hostages, provoke the terrorists or prejudice the negotiations. Alan Protheroe, the Editor of BBC TV News, has stated that he and his colleagues did maintain the closest contact with the police and that, while it was their function and duty to discover and transmit the news, their prime consideration throughout was to save lives; he did, however, complain that the police, while giving plenty of advice, gave the media too little information and that if they had taken the editors more into their confidence there would have been less rather than more transmission of information they would have preferred to keep quiet. He is almost certainly right as regards editors. On the other hand, Donald Trelford, Editor of the *Observer*, was doubtful about how far some journalists could be trusted, a few of them being cowboys who were only in it for a story. Protheroe, however, stressed that the trust should be given at editorial level, where the decision whether to transmit or publish was taken.[5]

The siege reached a climax on 5 May for the terrorists, the hostages, the police and the media. This was the sixth day of the siege. Even the police negotiators were showing signs of exhaustion, and there were four of them working in shifts. On the terrorist side, however, all the negotiations had been conducted by one man, Oan, the only one who spoke English and who was also their leader. He had, for the first three days, shown remarkable endurance and composure, but on the fourth day, he had become exasperated with the delay in broadcasting the statement of his aims. He had blamed the police for this rather than the media and had come very close to shooting one of the British hostages. By the sixth day, having achieved the publicity he wanted, he had abandoned all his demands other than for safe conduct out of the country. For this he demanded the mediation of one or more speci- fied Arab ambassadors but the British appeared to be stalling. In fact, it is now known that the Arab ambassadors concerned were unwilling to mediate unless they had a free hand to agree on behalf of the British Government to the demand for safe conduct, and the British Government were not willing to concede this.[6] Oan may have begun to sense that this was what was behind the continued stalling in the negotiation and by the morning of 5 May the tension in the Embassy was explosive.

At 11 a.m. PC Lock was instructed to tell the police negotiators through the window that, unless there was some firm news within 30 minutes of an Arab ambassador coming a hostage would be shot. Oan was persuaded to wait until he had listened to the midday news broadcasts but, when these produced nothing con- clusive, the terrorists tied up one of the hostages, Abbas Lavasani, close to the negotiating telephone, fired three shots and declared that they had shot him. This was at 1.45 p.m.

The police and the government's Crisis Committee concluded that the terrorists had decided to carry out their threat to kill hostages until they got their way. During an afternoon of intense activity outside, there was a mood of despair amongst both the hostages and the terrorists who clearly saw no other way out. This mood was detected by Professor Gunn, monitoring the telephone negotiations and (presumably) the conversations recorded by the surveillance microphones which must long since have been in- serted through the Embassy Walls. Oan was persuaded to wait for a personal message from Sir David McNee, the Metropolitan Police Commissioner, but when this arrived at 6 p.m. it said little more than that the police would not use violence unless the terror- ists did, and Oan furiously announced that he would kill one more hostage every 45 minutes until an Arab ambassador arrived. After 30 minutes of fruitless negotiation by the Iman of the London Central Mosque, more shots were heard and at 6.50 p.m. the body of Lavasani was pushed out of the front door.

THE SAS RAID

At this point, with positive proof that the terrorists had killed at
least one hostage and that they were virtually certain to kill more,
the Home Secretary decided to authorize the SAS, who had been
standing by with a plan at immediate readiness since the start of
the siege, to go in. This they did at 7.23 p.m. and within 11
minutes all the hostages were rescued alive except one whom the
terrorists shot dead during the attack. Five of the terrorists were
killed and the sixth (initially mistaken for a hostage) was captured.

It was when the SAS attack went in that a critical moment of
decision came for the two television news media — BBC TV News
and ITN.

The big cameras of their outside broadcast (OB) units, with
powerful telephoto lenses, were already installed facing the front
of the Embassy, with police approval, and were able to broadcast
live. The police, however, had asked the media not to position
cameras at the rear of the Embassy as they were anxious that the
terrorists should not know of the existence of certain surveillance
equipment which might unwittingly be revealed in camera shots
from the back. The police also knew (though the press did not)
that if the SAS were sent in their main assault would be made by
men abseiling down from the roof of the Embassy to enter by the
back windows. There was, of course, known to be a television set in
the Embassy and, if live pictures of the SAS men on the roof, or
descending on their ropes, had been seen by the terrorists even ten
seconds before they broke in, the result could have been disastrous. They did not in fact get this warning, but the danger was a
real one. This was proved by the fact that, as soon as the SAS exploded their first charge to break in, the terrorists began to spray
the hostages with their submachine guns, killing one more hostage
and wounding three others in the few seconds before they either
ran out of the room or (in some cases) tried to pretend they were
hostages. Given ten more seconds, or worse still a minute or two,
they would probably have killed all the hostages and some of the
SAS men before they were overwhelmed.

In defiance of the police request, an ITN cameraman posing as
a resident of a nearby block of flats had smuggled a hand-held
electronic camera, hidden in a suitcase, through the police cordon
covering the rear of the Embassy. He had established himself in
the window of a flat overlooking the rear of the Embassy and as

soon as the SAS men appeared on the roof and started to lower their ropes he switched on. The electronic camera transmits directly to the studio and its pictures technically could be (though currently were not) transmitted live, directly on to the television screens. In this case the pictures were displayed on monitors in the studio and recorded on videotape so that they could if required be retransmitted (like a football action replay) within a few seconds.

ITN was not itself on the air at 7.23 p.m. but the ITV programmes had a break for advertisements four minutes later and broadcast ITN pictures live (from their legitimate OB cameras at the front) or as action replays (the pictures from the illicit camera at the back). By this time, the SAS were already inside the Embassy. There had been a number of explosions as they blew in the bullet-proof windows and threw in stun grenades and flames were emerging from the building. The sounds of screams and shooting could be clearly heard and it was fair to assume that no one in the Embassy would by then be watching television, whether or not they had been doing so before, and that even if they were it would not influence their actions.

The editorial decision to broadcast live after four minutes may, in these circumstances, have been reasonable. The decision to smuggle in the camera in defiance of the police request, however, is not easy to justify. The police had given a good reason for this request as it was, and could hardly have been expected to tell the media of the second reason — that this was the way the SAS would attack if it were decided to mount a rescue operation. The SAS themselves, presumably, were acting on the assumption that there were no cameras recording their movements from the back.

Had the SAS attack happened to go in while an ITN bulletin was already being broadcast there would have been at least a possibility of the editor or studio director, unaware of the significance of the shots on the back camera videotape, switching them on to the transmitter before the SAS had actually gone through the windows, with potentially disastrous results. It can be argued that ITN's editors and directors are responsible people and would not have done this, which is probably true, but there was too much at stake to leave this to chance.

ITN expressed no regrets, and did not appear on the BBC *Editors* programme (already quoted) in which the decision was discussed. They were, however, staunchly defended on that programme by their BBC rival, Alan Protheroe, who commended their success in smuggling in the camera, and said that he wished the BBC had got one in too, even though he had deduced the main reason why the police did not wish them to do so. He said that the job of the media is 'quite simply, to disclose', though not necessarily to disclose immediately.

The BBC did not break into their programmes until eight minutes after the SAS attack went in. By that time they already had pictures of the two SAS men blowing their way in from the front, with the sounds of screaming and shooting from within and these, together with the live shots of hostages coming out and fire engines moving in, made dramatic viewing. Protheroe described it as 'one of the finest hours' of television. Those who saw it will never forget it. They saw history being made, like the American viewers in 1963 who suddenly found themselves watching, live, the murder of Lee Harvey Oswald, the alleged assassin of President Kennedy.

The murder of Lee Harvey Oswald happened quite unexpectedly and there was no time for an editorial decision — it was done and it went out live. At Prince's Gate, however, there was time for an editorial decision and it must be asked whether the additional drama and the 'duty to disclose' really justified the difference between four minutes or eight minutes or even thirty minutes. In fact, the police did not tell the media who had caused the explosion until forty minutes later, so it is not surprising that the first TV reports were confused though they fortunately did no harm. Once ITV had gone live, of course, the BBC could hardly be expected not to compete, but there was a much more coherent report on the main *News* at 9.50 p.m., by which time the police had given their press conference at 8.10 p.m. and there had been time to arrange the video tapes, film and commentary into a story. Viewers who saw only the coverage between 7 and 8 p.m. got a very confused and misleading picture, even if it did have the spice of, say, a live cup final, when the result still lay in the lap of the gods, as compared with *Match of the Day*, when the result is known.

The whole experience opens up another spectre — the possible future use of the electronic camera for live electronic news gathering (ENG) though the hand-held cameras in use with the rather more cumbersome OB units can already feed live pictures. There could, however, have been a terrible risk if the pictures from the illicit ITN camera at the back had been broadcasting live, so that the SAS were seen on the roof before anyone realized what they were doing — anyone, that is, except the terrorists watching their screen in the Embassy. This risk also applied, of course, to the OB cameras in front, but the police and the SAS knew they were there and acted accordingly.

Another hazard of live broadcasting of a battle of any kind (whether by normal OB units or ENG) is that a person in full tele-photo view might suddenly be split up the middle by a hand grenade. Though directors are trained to cope with this by cutting away etc., this could give a catastrophic and lasting shock to sensitive viewers, especially children.

The chief danger, however, remains that of causing loss of life by prejudicing negotiations or the success of a rescue operation. Neither the cut-throat competition for news nor the 'duty to disclose' could ever excuse anyone who knowingly or recklessly took that risk.

NEWS BLACK-OUTS

After watching the live coverage of the rescue Clive James, the *Observer* TV critic, called for a ban on the reporting of sieges where hostages' lives were at risk.[7] This may be justified but it would also have disadvantages, quite apart from the undesirability of blanket bans — the thin end of an ugly wedge. Such a ban would, of course, be imposed as a matter of course in the Soviet Union and any other totalitarian state. It can be cogently argued that that is why they have had so little terrorism, but the price of living in a society where the citizen is told only what the government decrees that he should be told is one which few people in a liberal democracy would wish to pay.

It is well established that the primary aim of most political terrorist attacks is publicity, and that if the media connive at this they are allowing themselves to be hijacked. Nevertheless, in countries where the overriding aim is to end a hostage situation without bloodshed on either side, this publicity is something which their governments, encouraged by their police forces, may be prepared to concede. The BBC's Managing Editor Tony Crabb went at police request precisely to convince the terrorists that their edited statement would be disseminated, and it was. Otherwise they had threatened to kill a hostage within 10 minutes and subsequent events leave little doubt that they would have done so. Appeasement may be dangerous but rigidity can be carried too far.[8]

Most news media, including the BBC and ITV, do have clearly written guidelines on meeting specific requests for news blackouts. In the case of the BBC, the principle is that information may be withheld as part of a recognized embargo arrangement, to avoid the distress to next of kin who might learn of a bereavement for the first time over the air, or where human life could be endangered by premature publicity. Account is taken of the motives for the request and if there is a political motive it will carry less weight than a private family one. Obviously the question of whether the incident has already become public knowledge (as is usually the case with either a hijacking or a siege) will weigh heavily.

The media in Britain are, in addition, liable for criminal charges if, during a hijack or siege where lives are at risk, they rebroadcast any internal VHF traffic (e.g. between police officers or between the control tower and aircraft), whether or not this is in itself useful to the terrorist. The D Notice Committee could also, if it judged fit, issue a request for a black-out but D Notice requests are not in themselves legally binding.

Sir Robert Mark, a pioneer in the field of police–press relations, accepted that the onus was on the police to justify any black-out request they might make; that it must only be made if human lives would otherwise be put in jeopardy; that the request must lapse after 48 hours unless specifically renewed; and that reporters should be fully and regularly briefed, with as much background as possible on the reasons for the request. He also accepted that the fact that the news was temporarily blacked out did not constitute an embargo on journalistic activity to acquire that news in readiness to publish it later.

In an earlier BBC *Editors* programme, Sir Robert Mark faced a discussion with a number of editors including Larry Lamb, of the *Sun* and the *News of the World*. The chairman (George Scott) asked Larry Lamb whether, if Sir Robert were to ask him to withhold a piece of information but said he was unable to explain why, he would accept the request.

'Without hesitation', he said.

'Would you do the same for any Chief Constable?'

'Certainly not, but I know that Sir Robert would not ask me unless lives were at risk, and that is all I need to know to agree to the request.'

This underlines that the most important single factor is mutual trust between the police and the editors and extended by them where possible to their reporters. An indispensable ingredient in this is either first-hand knowledge of the other person or endorsement by someone who is known and personally trusted by both sides. If such trust can be established, together with instant communications between the ground, the studio or the newsroom, it will be more effective in the end than legal constraints. Conscience aside, no journalist, newspaper or broadcasting organization can afford to get a reputation for being untrustworthy or, still worse, to be seen to have wantonly caused loss of life by failing to heed a warning or reasonable request.

At the same time, however, editors, producers and journalists have a duty to minimize risks to their own colleagues, particularly if one of them is himself a hostage, as at Prince's Gate. The same applies if, as in a sadly large number of countries, journalists are liable to physical attack or intimidation. Sometimes an editor may feel that if he complies with a police request to publish or not to publish a statement or news item, this could be misinterpreted by the terrorists as a response to their own coercion or intimidation and could therefore create a dangerous precedent. This may provide another reason for an editor to be reluctant to agree to a police request. Once again, if such dilemmas are to be resolved, there is no substitute for mutual confidence and trust between the police and the media and a willingness by each to understand both the issues involved and the needs of the other. A journalist who knowingly deceives the police and betrays this trust may not only place lives at risk, but thereby also prejudice the chances of other journalists being taken into the confidence of the police in future.

Part IV
What is to be Done?

What Is to me Done?

14 Living with the Media

THE IMPORTANCE OF BEING INTERVIEWED

The main body of this book has been concerned with the ways in which political violence of every kind poisons and erodes the functioning of a parliamentary democratic society, and the ways in which the media have helped or hindered in containing the violence and in preserving that society. We have seen how political activists can exploit internal conflicts and use the media to further their aims. The whole basis of pluralism is freedom of expression of differing opinions which is why every Marxist or fascist country has had to supplant editorial freedom by party control, either through the state apparatus or through a union controlled by the party. By definition, those who wish to live in a free society must accept a free press and must develop the art of living with it.

Denis MacShane's book *Using the Media*[1] is a superb guide for the political activist. He makes no bones about his Marxist philosophy, as quoted earlier,[2] and the first words of his book state its purpose:

'This handbook is designed to equip:
   workers
   trade union officials
   community activists
   local political activists
   pressure groups
for the most effective use of the media'.[3]

Denis MacShane is, among other things, a tutor on the TUC's courses on 'using the media' and the professionalism he teaches will be valuable to anyone, whether in his listed categories or not. The aim of this chapter is to help those who wish to preserve a pluralist society and, as part of it, editorial freedom of the media, to apply this same professionalism in using the media to that end.

147

There are similar courses run for industry and business. Some other institutions, such as the army and the police, run their own. This chapter cannot replace such courses. It is written primarily to assist those who are representatives of organizations and institutions, public, social, industrial or commercial, who may find themselves asked for interviews or who wish to take the initiative in getting their views into the press or on radio or television.

Being interviewed can be an ordeal but it is much more often a stimulus and a pleasure. I have decided to lapse into the first and second person because I shall be discussing it mainly from my own experience and can look at it from the point of view of the victim rather than of the journalist. My aim, therefore, is to pass on this experience to other potential victims in the hope that they too can sit back and enjoy it.

I first appeared on television in 1970, while I was a soldier, and there was just time for me to fit in the army's excellent television orientation course before I did so; since then I have taken part in about 140 broadcasts, 60 on television and 80 on radio, varying from 45-minute discussions to two-minute comments on the news. Four have been with that past master of the art, Sir Robin Day, and the one I enjoyed most was when he refereed a 15-minute TV confrontation with Arthur Scargill.[4]

Amongst press interviews, the most substantial one required me to share my life and work for two days with E. J. Kahn, Jr, of the *New Yorker* from which he wrote a 7000 word profile,[5] expounding my views better than I could ever have expounded them myself. The other end of the scale has been to answer hectic telephone calls from a reporter wanting to quote a fact or an opinion a few minutes before his deadline.

NEWSPAPERS AND JOURNALS

The big news agencies (AP, Reuter, PA, UPI) and the newspapers themselves, run both a permanent staff of journalists and several thousand 'stringers' or freelance journalists all over the world from whom they can request information or who can send in copy by telephone when something happens. These journalists, staff or freelance, get most of their information by talking to members of the public involved or by telephoning people who are in official positions or who may have expert knowledge. They will be very sensitive about time, accuracy and exclusiveness. They cannot afford to miss a deadline or to be proved wrong. They will therefore cultivate their links with people whom they can trust to give them reliable information or an authoritative interpretation quickly, sometimes a private individual, sometimes a representative of an institution. Such a link can be of immense value to both sides because, once it is established, the journalist will not hazard it by betraying a trust or breaking an agreement for a conversation to be non-attributable or off the record. If you can establish such a link it will give you a channel to the media which you in turn can trust.

Everything a reporter writes, however, has to be subedited, to fit in the space available, to tie in with other items, etc. The headline, also, will usually be written by someone other than the reporter. These things can, through no fault of the reporter, radically change the slant or balance of his piece, and all you can do is to make your statements sufficiently simple and explicit not to be vulnerable to them. If you suspect that there may be a hostile or deliberately misleading headline, you should be wary of being quoted at all in the paper concerned.

The same considerations apply to a personal interview as to a telephone call, but the interview will usually be by appointment so there will have been time for some homework. It is always wise to agree in advance on the questions or at least on the ground to be covered.

Because of the constraints of time and subediting, it is a rare privilege to be allowed to check the reporter's draft before it goes to press. In special cases it may be worth asking. The more you can establish a prospect of being a valuable contact in the future, the more likely you are to be given this privilege, even if only by a quick reading over the telephone. In preparing the 7000-word profile for the *New Yorker* mentioned above, a subeditor consumed some eight hours of transatlantic telephone time checking it both for accuracy and for shades of meaning, but this must be very rare. Journalists on the *Daily Telegraph*, the *Daily Mirror* and the *Observer* have also checked drafts with me on occasions but this has always been with a reporter with whom I have built up a personal relationship over a period. It is possible to make an interview conditional upon approving the draft, but this is very seldom either wise or reasonable. Trust, and something to lose on both sides, give much better safeguards.

It is considerably more difficult to take the initiative yourself in getting into print. Pressure on the correspondence columns of national papers, especially *The Times*, is very heavy and the best chance lies in a brief but controversial letter which is likely to provoke further interesting correspondence. Much the same applies to unsolicited articles. Once again, a better way may be to cultivate the acquaintance of a successful journalist who will welcome well-informed ideas for an article.

In cultivating such a relationship it is important to remember not only the constraints but also the motivations of a journalist, which have been touched upon throughout this book. His reputation, and hence his future opportunities, will depend on his writing timely, accurate and original pieces which will attract readers to him and to his paper in the future. It is no use expecting him to write stuff which will bore his readers or which his editor will not print. If, however, you can help him to get what he needs in order to write what he wants, you will become a valued friend and he will be no less valuable a friend to you.

RADIO AND TV NEWS AND CURRENT AFFAIRS

Before discussing the arts and techniques of facing television interviews, it may be useful to identify some of the staff involved in making news and current affairs programmes. This varies considerably between the BBC and different ITV programme companies, and also between different BBC programmes.

For programmes like the BBC's *Panorama* or *Newsweek*, the most important man is the *editor*. He plans usually several weeks and sometimes several months ahead, the subjects for future programmes. He allocates each to a *producer* who may have an assistant and one or more production assistants who set up the programme with the studio teams, or, if appropriate, with an outside broadcast or film unit. The producer may also be assisted by one or more *researchers*. These are the junior members of the team, the best of whom will be the producers and editors of the future. They will have been hand-picked from literally hundreds of applicants and are usually very intelligent and stimulating people. They have to make their names by delivering the goods — the goods being the right person to be interviewed, prepared to answer the questions the producer wants. This may be a distinguished public figure (though the producer will in that case probably prepare the way by a letter or telephone call as a matter of courtesy). The researcher may, however, simply be asked to go to, say, a factory or housing area, find some representative and articulate people and run over the ground with them. A common approach is to say 'we are planning a programme . . . could I ask your advice?' and then, if from the conversation it seems that you will be a good subject, a specific date will be made for a visit by a film crew or for you to attend a studio interview. The researcher, however, will probably have to refer the proposals to a producer or editor. Do not expect an on-the-spot guarantee that you will or will not appear with a certain other person or that certain questions will not be asked. The researcher can only recommend, not decide.

A researcher works in a competitive world and, if you can help to find either the information required or some other interesting person to interview, you will earn gratitude and consequently a fair wind from the start.

The researcher's task will also overlap the work of the *reporter* who may often have a very free hand in both the investigation and the writing of a story, though the producer will have the final say in editing and deciding what does and does not go in. Your first approach may come direct from the reporter who will do the interview. Occasionally, a researcher may come with a film crew to ask the questions which will then be dubbed in by the interviewer, or your answers simply worked into the programme without a question.

Reporters are usually experienced journalists who have learned their trade on a newspaper. They will very often be considerably older than their producers and even than their editors. Producers and editors are the future senior managers in the BBC or ITV hierarchy. To apply an army analogy, they are the captains and majors, who must be young enough to become colonels and generals before they are too long in the tooth. Their job is also essentially active and creative. Most producers are in their twenties and editors in their thirties. Roger Bolton became Editor of *Panorama* at 32. There is sometimes some edginess between the whizz-kids and the more experienced reporters. You should bear this in mind and be diplomatic.

The *presenter*, or anchorman, will also be an experienced journalist but is unlikely to have direct contact with the interviewee unless the programme contains a major studio discussion which he chairs or a particularly important interview which he does himself. Practices vary. In *Newsweek*, for example, the reporter goes out and does the filming and then presents the programme, including any studio discussions, himself.

In a magazine programme like *Nationwide* the gestation period for an interview is obviously shorter than for *Panorama*, *World in Action*, *Newsweek* or *Weekend World*. You are likely to be telephoned in the morning or even mid-afternoon and asked to appear that evening, perhaps having to do so from a regional studio by landline, of which more later.

The structure of a news programme is fairly similar but obviously everything moves faster still. The approach is likely to come direct from the reporter or sometimes from a researcher, and will probably be for an immediate interview, sometimes by telephone. You may, alternatively, get a call from a member of the news staff, seeking some facts or interpretations to feed into the news bulletin itself. You are fully entitled to require the information to be non-attributable, but it is usually worth taking any opportunity to ensure that the facts or perspectives are correct and it is valuable to build a reputation for being knowledgeable and ready to speak.

It is equally important to build a reputation for speaking the truth, and for being frank, especially if you are representing a big institution. The problems of the police and the army in this respect are discussed in the Northern Ireland context in Chapters 9 and 10. The lessons they learned and the techniques they developed are worth studying by other institutions. An unpleasant truth is going to come out in the end so it is best to face up to it as soon as you are sure of the facts.

Do not, incidentally, expect a fee for a news interview, whether as a spokesman or as a private individual. For a current affairs interview you may be offered a small fee (usually about £15–£20 in 1980) and more for a longer studio discussion (£50?). BBC and ITV will also pay your travelling expenses. Famous (or notorious) people may demand, and get, very much larger fees, but most people do not take part in news or current affairs programmes with the primary objective of making money.

TV DOCUMENTARIES AND DRAMA

As shown in Chapter 7, the influence of a TV documentary or

drama may be greater and more lasting than that of a news or current affairs programme. Experts or people involved in an organization or in a business may well be asked to advise in a production on their subject. It is important to try to detect early on whether the programme is likely to be biased in any particular direction and whether you want to be associated with it. If you are in any kind of official position and decline on behalf of your organization to take part you can be sure that the programme makers will mention this fact. You must balance the damage done by the implications of this with the less predictable damage which might be done by taking part, particularly if they are planning to use you as a 'fall guy'. In one very hostile documentary about the Prison Service, in which ex-convicts and the families of prisoners inside were given full rein to attack the system, the Prison Service declined to take part, but an official of the Prison Officers' Association did agree to comment at the end, and he was filmed in the most unfavourable setting at the far end of a long committee room with all the chairs empty, symbolizing that he spoke for no one. This was the worst of both worlds.

Generally it is better to take part, even if you sense that the intent may be hostile, provided that you are confident that you can prevent the interviewer from making a fool of you. If you hit back forcefully and concisely, they will probably include what you say because controversy makes for good television. If you are asked only to advise during production you can, if you wish, insist that your advice is non-attributable and that you are not named in the programme credits. It is better to try to get the facts straight, even anonymously, than to let them go by default.

Best of all, however, is for an organization or institution, public or private, to establish an atmosphere of open-handed co-operation from the start. Your contacts, as in current affairs, may be with a researcher, a producer, a reporter and a presenter. In the case of drama, you may also meet the author and possibly the director, who handles the artistic design and the positioning of cameras, backgrounds, etc., which can be very important.

Such co-operation was clearly established by the Metropolitan Police in the making of the documentary *Police–Harrow Road*.[6] The Royal Navy did the same with *Sailor* in 1975. They turned the BBC team loose in HMS *Ark Royal* for a complete cruise, with no provisos other than the right to exclude photographs of secret equipment. The Admiralty almost had kittens when the first of the ten-part series consisted not merely of 'warts and all' but of 'all warts', including the sailors' last night ashore and their alter-cations with the Petty Officers at the head of the gangway as they rolled back on board. The effect, however, was dramatic and hooked the audience, convincing them that this was *not* just a puff piece engineered by the Navy. The series was shown at a peak viewing time (9.25 p.m. on Thursdays) and started with an audience of 5 million, expanding to 9½ and 10 million for each of the last four episodes. It was repeated, again with audiences of up to 8 million, in 1977.

The army co-operated in the same way at Sandhurst with *The New Officers* in 1975 (a *Panorama* Special) and a series of four programmes about the Staff College in *War School* in 1979–80. In the same years Radley College lived with the cameras for months to enable the BBC to produce the ten-part *Public School* series and emerged with some bruises but an overwhelming balance of credit.

The Services also co-operated in a number of drama series. *Warship* began in 1973 with a 13-part series watched by an average of 12 million to 14 million, placing it amongst the very top programmes (it was very rare at that time for a programme to attract more than 18 million viewers). Further *Warship* series continued until 1977. The army co-operated, again with excellent results, in *Danger UXB* and *Spearhead*, which ran from 1976–9. The *Daily Telegraph* observed that '. . . *Spearhead* . . . has done for the Army what *Rumpole* is doing for lawyers and *All Creatures Great and Small* did for vets — giving a favourable fictional image without departing too far from documentary truth'.[7]

Major industries and other institutions have also successfully co-operated in TV drama and documentary series, notably the oil industry. Many others, big and small, have opened their doors for programmes such as *The Money Programme* and *The Risk Business*. It is possible to get a bloody nose, but rare. Whole-hearted co-operation almost invariably earns a substantial credit balance.

RADIO AND TELEVISION INTERVIEWS

Some people dismiss the value of radio and television interviews on the grounds that they are too short to cover any subject adequately. This betrays a misunderstanding of the nature and powers of broadcasting. If a man faces the cameras for even two or three minutes he can get across one vital point, or at most three or four. It is a mistake to try to cover too many. Just one point, well put, can make an impact on 5 million or 10 million people. This may be at least as effective as 1000 words reaching a million people in a newspaper article, or 3000 words reaching 50 000 discerning readers of a quality weekly, or 7000 words reaching a few hundred in an academic quarterly. Because of the impact of a picture, even of an expressive talking head, and because the viewer can judge sincerity and conviction when he sees it on the screen, a well-put remark on TV can have the most lasting effect of all.

The first problem is whether to accept, and this has already been discussed. It is generally better to take part than to let your case go by default, but only if you are satisfied that you know enough about the subject to talk about it and are willing to answer most, if not all, of the questions the interviewer intends to ask. You must always try to agree on those questions in advance. If there are some you are not willing to discuss you should say so and say why. The interviewer will usually accept this but it can go wrong (see, for example pages 130 and 174).

You should also ask whether you will be doing an interview jointly with someone else, or separately, and who, if anyone, will be interviewed before and after you. Also, find out whether it is to be live or recorded. Recording may seem safer in that, if there is an awkward question or if you have let slip something you would rather not have said you may be able to ask the producer to cut it out or, *in extremis*, force him to do so by yelling out a four letter word (as Denis Mac-Shane suggests[8]). On the whole, however, it is better to broadcast live, especially on controversial subjects so that, if you think it essential to correct or refute something you can do so, forcefully and persistently, without the risk of it being cut out by the editor's scissors.

Experienced performers can sometimes sense where those scissors may cut and take action to pre-empt them. One former Prime Minister, annoyed by his experience of having, for example, a qualifying phrase or sentence cut out of the tape, became adept at preventing this by avoiding the kind of 'cadence' which editors need if they are to cut. As he approached the end of a sentence at such a point he would suddenly raise his pitch and run straight on into the next sentence, so it was very difficult to cut him at all. Producers and interviewers hated him but they knew they were up against a professional.

The most hazardous programmes are those in which separate interviews are filmed at length, and short excerpts extracted to fit into the pattern the producer wants. To give an example, I once did such an interview for *World in Action* in which, after a three-hour preliminary discussion with the producer and researcher, followed by four hours over dinner with the interviewer, I spent two hours next morning (not shooting all the time) in front of the camera. The interviewer wanted two one-minute clips and had a very clear idea what he wanted me to say. In some cases he did five retakes of the answer to the same question. I kept the scissors in mind and tried to ensure that there were no passages which, cut out of context, could have a meaning I did not intend, but it was a risky game which I would not wish to play too often.

If possible, do the interview face to face rather than by landline and earplug from a different studio. Apart from anything else, you seem more natural when you are looking at the interviewer. If you look at the camera you may look popeyed or intense. If you watch the interviewer on the monitor screen in your studio you will find yourself looking at your own face, half sideways, just as you begin to answer. This will not only be disconcerting but will also make you look shifty (you should never look downwards in front of the camera). Earplugs can come adrift at critical moments. Also, when you are not switched in and someone is saying something wrong from another studio, you have no way of butting in (see, again, page 174).

It is also important to be positive and concise. This is especially important in a recording, because, if you are long-winded, your statement may be removed altogether or cut in such a way as to weaken it or take it out of context. Think about the total time available or (in a discussion) the amount of time the producer will want to allocate to you, and make sure that your essential points — one, two, three — get home. If they are pithy and short they will be used.

This underlines the vital importance of homework before any interview, especially before a television interview. You should be prepared in two ways: first, you should be ready to drive home your few selected key points and to seize the right opportunity to do so; secondly, you should be ready to answer (or if necessary to divert) the most likely and difficult questions you may face. This is particularly important in a discussion in which you will have adversaries. In that case you should also do the homework to take the initiative and throw them on to the defensive. You will never cover all the points you prepare but you must prepare on every front. It is quite useful to take notes into the studio but be careful never to look at them when the camera is on you. It is best if possible to memorize your points and never to look down at all.

The most important is the answer to the first question. Even if he is evasive about the other questions, the interviewer will usually tell you what the first one is going to be because it is in his interest to get the discussion off to a positive and incisive start. Your answer should set the tone for the whole interview.

Thereafter, keep to the agreed subject. If the interviewer or another participant tries to depart from that it is not difficult to divert. Every politician does it − e.g. 'that is an interesting point but before we discuss it we must first deal with . . .'. It is sometimes better to counter-attack, especially if it is someone you need to discredit − e.g. 'you keep trying to run away from the subject. What we were saying was . . .' − but avoid being rude or abrasive. Under no circumstances whatever must you lose your temper or your self-control, and you must avoid getting involved in discussing any subject if you do not know enough to handle it.

Finally, keep the time always at the back of your mind so that you can end the discussion on the right note. Ask the interviewer how long the whole discussion will be. There may be a studio clock. Avoid being caught looking at your watch, and put it on the table if you think you will need it. Get to know the studio manager's time signals. He will stand beside the camera which the interviewer can most easily see. One finger up means one minute to go. Crossed arms means 30 seconds. Winding a mangle means wrap up the discussion. The 'cut throat sign' means that the interviewer must cut in, whoever is speaking, and end the interview. If you can get the discussion on to the note you want during the last 30 seconds or wrap-up stage, what you say is what will stick in the viewer's mind.

15 The Media in a Reasonable Society

SUMMARY OF CONCLUSIONS FROM THE CASE-STUDIES

In the Introduction to this book attention was drawn to the link between editorial freedom of the media and the low level of political violence in Britain; and to the necessity of preserving both of these things if we are to maintain the tranquillity of a pluralist and tolerant society under the rule of law.

Part I of the book looked at the influence of the media on industrial disputes and especially on the prospects of violence on picket lines. The case-studies suggest that the media generally reflect the views of the public, which dislikes strikes and especially strikes of public services and violent picketing. Television news reports, especially, appear to be less biased than the public themselves, but any bias against strikers arouses a sense of injustice and increases the likelihood of frustration exploding into violence. The media by their nature record the highlights and these tend to be the relatively rare outbreaks of violence which are not typical. This adds further weight to the feeling amongst strikers that the media are being unfair to them. While the presence of the camera may encourage some pickets to act up, the exposure of excessive violence can make it counter-productive and so deter it.

The bare reporting of news of picketing incidents tends to reinforce the prejudices on both sides. The media can mitigate this by providing better coverage of the background to a dispute. They may also be able to restrain the conflict by giving a fuller analysis of the longer-term cost of the dispute to the strikers, to the firms, to job prospects, to the national economy and to the consumer, since this may encourage both sides to be more reasonable.

Industrial disputes and unemployment can be exploited for purely political motives by people outside the trade union movement. Their aim may be primarily to gain publicity for fringe political movements or to provoke a violent situation in order to discredit the police. The media should be aware of these motives and avoid being used as a tool.

Racial conflict is the other issue most commonly exploited for political demonstrations. Because of the intensity of feeling on both sides in areas with a large immigrant population, this provides an explosive mixture, easy to ignite. Again the media should show responsibility and avoid exacerbating the conflict or being used as a tool by people seeking publicity. Rather than use conspicuous cameras (e.g. on roofs) and floodlights, the discreet use of hand-held cameras as described on page 82 has proved a sensible idea.

While it is not in the public interest to glorify violence or those who use it, the media must give coverage to violent demonstrations, because they are news about which the public has a right to know. The exposure of the violence usually reacts in the end against its instigators. Moreover, since one of the aims of the violence is to gain publicity, the denial of it may encourage the use of still greater violence to attract it. The totalitarian alternative of total censorship of reports of civil unrest is far more unhealthy, and inconsistent with a reasonable society.

Another aim of the violence may be to discredit the police by provoking overreaction. Some senior police officers welcome the presence of cameras because they may restrain individual policemen from using more than the minimum necessary force.

There have been accusations by MPs and senior police officers (see pages 65 and 66–9) that the media, and the BBC in particular, have been parties to a concerted campaign to discredit the police. There are some grounds for this accusation, though it is probably exaggerated, certainly in the case of news and current affairs reporting. There is more cause for concern over documentaries and drama presentations about the police, the prison services and the institutions of the law. Fiction is a valuable medium for exposing abuses and may do so more faithfully and effectively than factual reporting. Nevertheless, some authors and producers avowedly use their access to the media to weaken the rule of law in order to make way for political change, and depart from dramatic truth – i.e., present false propaganda – with this intent. The BBC should be less naive than it sometimes is in making available prime television time for dishonest propaganda in the guise of drama or documentaries.

Reporting violence in Northern Ireland presents particular problems and demands a particularly high sense of responsibility. This may be lacking in some young reporters trying to make their names and ready to turn a blind eye to hazarding lives to get a good story. The IRA and its legal political organization, Sinn Fein, are adept at using these reporters for their propaganda. The government, police and army must counter this by always telling the truth, with care to be sure of the facts before making a statement. This need for accuracy may give the terrorists the advantage of getting in first with their story and they exploit this to the full. Again, the media have often been gullible in allowing themselves to be used.

Some journalists and politicians have put a strong case for giving the terrorists themselves access to the media in the form of personal television interviews. Their main arguments are that the public need to see the terrorists for what they are, and that denial of such access will lead them to try to grab the news with more spectacular violence. These arguments are outweighed by the arguments against giving publicity and a propaganda platform to criminals. The public gained nothing from the interview with the INLA who claimed to have murdered Airey Neave, but the INLA gained immense publicity and prestige. It is also likely that this publicity coup goaded the IRA into matching it by murdering Earl Mountbatten. Television interviews with terrorists, operating in the UK, or with spokesmen for illegal and criminal organizations, whether facing or back to camera, should never be given.

Virtually all the British media were grossly irresponsible in the early stages of the kidnapping of the Schild family in Sardinia, though they made up for it by laudable restraint during the last two months of the case. They should have followed the example of the Italian media, which have learned by bitter experience not to hazard the lives of kidnap victims by irresponsible reporting and conjecture.

A similar sense of responsibility is needed in covering siege situations such as that of the Iranian Embassy in London in 1980. The police on such occasions must tell the media all that they can and must then trust them — and be trusted by them. This trust was deliberately broken by one television cameraman. Had the rescue attempt chanced to begin while a news bulletin was in progress, this could have resulted in the death of all the hostages. It was lucky that it did not do so, but this does not excuse the cameraman or his editors for deliberately deceiving the police and disregarding their instructions when lives were clearly at risk.

VOLUNTARY CONTROL OR LEGISLATION?

The best answer to this kind of irresponsible or anti-social misuse of the power of the media lies in the hands of the journalistic profession itself. The Press Council (for editors), the Institute of Journalists and the National Union of Journalists all have certain codes which their members are obliged to observe at pain of expulsion. These should be strengthened and enforced.

There is, however, a need for something wider than any of these, an Institute for the Mass Media (IMM) on the lines of the British Medical Association (BMA) or the Bar or the Law Society. The IMM (though not, of course, its individual members) would be barred by its Charter from political activity, just as the trade unions are in Germany. Its members would initially be confined to anyone involved in *editorial decisions in a mass medium* which would be defined as any newspaper or journal with a circulation of more than, say, 100 000 and any licensed broadcasting station, radio or television. Those involved in 'editorial decisions' would include anyone in a position to approve, or to insert or reword, material for publication or broadcasting. They would therefore include, not only editors and subeditors, but also newsreaders, presenters and producers. Later, as the IMM developed, it should include all journalists on the staff of the mass media, though it would be neither practicable nor desirable to include freelance or lay contributors, or editors or journalists working for small local papers, low-circulation newspapers (such as *Morning Star* or *Socialist Worker*) or any but the largest national weeklies and monthlies.

Everyone involved in the editorial process of the mass media would be required to be a registered member of the IMM and breach of its code would result in the offender being struck off the Register. In that case he would be barred from practising in that capacity (though he could earn his living instead on a smaller paper) in the same way that a doctor is barred from practising if he is struck off the Register. Lawyers and chartered engineers are other examples of professions in which practice is conditional on observing a professional code. Anyone able to release material to the presses or transmitters of a national newspaper or radio or, most of all, television, has considerably more power to damage the community than a doctor, lawyer or engineer.

Registered members of the IMM would also be required, subject to appeal to a court or tribunal, to cease to employ or to publish in the defined mass media the work of any journalist or contributor who had knowingly broken the code.

The code would include most of what is already in the codes of the Press Association, IOJ and NUJ. In relation to the problem of placing lives at risk the relevant code should be:

> Any person who wilfully or recklessly misuses his position as an editor or journalist on a mass medium of communication in such a way as to place lives at risk or facilitate the escape of a person wanted for an indictable criminal offence shall be struck off the Register.

As the IMM develops it might be desirable to widen this to include cameramen and others involved in the production of news. It should also include

> any person who, while acting as an editor or journalist on a mass medium of communication knowingly disobeys, or connives at the disobedience of, police instructions in a situation in which the police have stated that lives are at risk.

If the profession is unable or unwilling to introduce such a system, or fails to enforce it, then the same offences should be made into criminal offences. The parallel in this case is the offence of 'reckless driving'. The reckless driver does not have to kill anyone, or even to hit anything, to be found guilty. He merely has to handle his vehicle recklessly. A television camera can be at least as lethal as a car.

A LOCAL STATE OF EMERGENCY

The development of the IMM and the extension of its control to every mass medium of communication would take time. The alternative of legislation should be introduced only if this fails, and that, too would take time.

Meanwhile, temporary legislation should be introduced to enable a Chief Constable to declare a Local State of Emergency at his discretion, for a period not to exceed six hours unless its continuation is authorized by the Home Office on the advice of the Police Authority. This could usefully be applied to situations such as natural disasters as well as to terrorist incidents. The offences described above would be incorporated in the appropriate Enabling Act.

RESPONSIBILITY TO A REASONABLE SOCIETY

The handling of terrorism is only one aspect of the much wider requirement for journalistic responsibility in a reasonable society which protects freedom of the media. The protection of this freedom should be incorporated in the code of the IMM, though it would require careful drafting to avoid it being restrictive of the free expression of the full range of political opinion from extreme right to extreme left provided that it falls within the law.

As set out at the start of this book, it would also be detrimental to the health of a pluralist society, and a denial of its essential nature, to inhibit the journalistic scrutiny of public institutions, subject to the normal safeguards of security and freedom from unreasonable harassment. Investigative journalism is the best guard against corruption and other abuses which can be a fatal disease in a parliamentary democracy.

Nevertheless, in exposing the rotten apples, the IMM's ethical code should require a journalist to show good faith and to put his disclosures in fair perspective. This would be a matter for the Council or Court of the Institute to judge, as in the case of the GMC and a doctor accused of improper conduct.

In any civilized society, citizens are required to observe the law, which in turn requires reasonable consideration for the rights of others. Personal freedom ultimately depends upon free media to which the individual can turn to publicize his plight or his grievance, but the free media must show reasonable consideration for the community if their freedom is to survive.

Consideration for the community includes a *moral* obligation on those who wish to retain freedom of the media to preserve the parliamentary democracy and rule of law upon which that freedom depends.

This obligation can only be a moral one, and the best way of removing those whose views they abhor is for readers, listeners or viewers to switch to another paper or another channel. The normal pressures of a free press will then drive the editor to exercise his editorial freedom not to publish material which bores or alienates his public. Those who oppose parliamentary democracy must retain the right to express their opposition in the media, but whether they have space to do so in the *mass* media must depend upon a free editorial decision which in turn depends on what the editor judges is in keeping with the wishes of his public. If readers of the mass media do not want to read their work they must be content, like others, with access to media with minority readership whose editors will publish it. The public are the best judges of the hypocrisy of the fascist or Marxist who claims the right of freedom of expression as a vehicle for persuading the people to follow his lead when he well knows that no fascist or Marxist society in the world permits freedom of the press or investigative journalism. Nevertheless, hypocritical or not, his right to promote these views must be respected or the society cannot call itself either reasonable or free. The most important freedom of all to protect, however, is editorial freedom, to publish or not to publish, under the guidance of the public's free choice.

Apart from the tiny proportion who reject the democratic society — and this does include a number of the writers and journalists whose work is quoted in this book — other journalists should not be ashamed to show in their work a support for the reasonable society, exercising the freedom it gives them to disclose its shortcomings and abuses in order to strengthen it. If they believe in it, and believe that the majority of the public wants it, they should ask themselves in each case whether their action will on balance help or hinder its survival. The quotation of Sir Ian Trethowan on page 83 gives the best guide to the principles involved.

These principles should apply particularly to all those involved in the production of news and other programmes on television. In the battle for survival of the reasonable society the television camera is the super tank — the Queen of the Battlefield. Ordinary mortals are wise to learn her ways and treat her with respect, but those who serve in her entourage have an awful responsibility.

Notes and References

INTRODUCTION

1. The Observer, *Siege* (London: Macmillan, 1980).
2. For more detailed proposals for restoring power to the people through Parliament, see Richard Clutterbuck, *Britain in Agony* (Harmondsworth: Penguin, 1980) pp. 280–96.
3. Robin Day, *Day by Day* (London: William Kimber, 1975) p. 54.
4. There is, however, an element of cynicism and dishonesty in the declaration of the sanctity of freedom of the press by some of the journalists who use that freedom to 'propagate a very different set of ideas' because they know well enough that journalists have invariably lost that freedom in the kind of society they envisage. What they really seek is not freedom but *control* of the media, avowedly in the name of the people, by their own elite political party. The most feasible and insidious way of bringing this about would be to establish a journalists' union closed shop, under the control of that elite, of which all *editors* as well as journalists would be obliged to be members. Editors would then be subject to dismissal from the union (and thus from their jobs) if they were judged to have 'acted in a manner detrimental to the interests of the union'. Party control of that union would thus be tantamount to editorial control of all the mass media. If (as at present) the state were not already a one-party dictatorship, this control would be the most important step towards making it so. Editorial freedom acts not only as the prime guardian of individual liberty by exposing abuses by the state, but is also an indispensable safeguard for the survival of the democratic system which allows editorial freedom itself. This threat to editorial freedom implied in Michael Foot's Closed Shop Bill in 1976, was exposed by Nora Beloff in *Freedom Under Foot* (London: Temple Smith, 1976).
5. Sir Ian Trethowan's view is quoted in full on page 83.
6. *Listener*, 4 August 1977.
7. Robin Day, *Day by Day*, pp. 54–5. He expanded further on the same theme in his interview with Bernard Levin on BBC2, *The Levin Interviews*, 3 May 1980 in which he said that he could see no grievance in Great Britain which justified the use of violence.
8. Lord Scarman, interview, 12 December 1977.

CHAPTER 1: A BIAS AGAINST THE UNIONS?

1. This shop steward was a member of the Communist Party. He was well

known as a political and industrial militant but personally a responsible and compassionate man. It was something of a surprise to find him advocating the provocation of violence to arouse hatred and was a reminder of the power of ideology. For a fuller exposition of his views see Richard Clutterbuck, *Britain in Agony*, pp. 245–8 and 343.

2. TUC Publication, London, 1979.
3. TUC Publication, London, 1979.
4. Peter Beharrell and Greg Philo (eds), *Trade Unions and the Media* (London: Macmillan, 1977) p. 8. The same two writers were members of the Glasgow Media Group which wrote *Bad News* (1976) and *More Bad News* (1980) which were mentioned in the Introduction.
5. Denis MacShane, *Using the Media: Workers' Handbook* (London: Pluto Press, 1979) p. 1.
6. See page 8 above.
7. Estimates calculated from tables in *Bad News*, p. 3.
8. See Clutterbuck, *Britain in Agony*, p. 197.
9. Calculated from 1978 readership figures quoted in MacShane, *Using the Media*, p. 14.
10. *A Cause for Concern*, p. 19.
11. e.g. See *Mirror* headline quoted in TUC, *A Cause for Concern*, p. 20. The pamphlet also complains (p. 19) that some strikers (e.g. nurses) receive more sympathetic media treatment than others, but this is again a reflection of the sympathies of the public.
12. 1978 circulation figures from MacShane, *Using the Media*, p. 15.

CHAPTER 2: THE BATTLE OF SALTLEY, 1972

1. For an account of this strike see Clutterbuck, *Britain in Agony*, chs 3 and 4.
2. See Alfred Robens, *Ten Year Stint* (London: Cassell, 1972).
3. This compassion amongst trade unionists largely vanished during the 1970s, and was probably a casualty of the affluent society, and of a rising level of social security payments. Trade union leaders competing for support became more ruthless in their insistence on maximum increases for their own members regardless of the unemployment this would cause others. The cutbacks in the coal, steel and motor industries, plus the growth of inflation and unemployment and the decline of the British economy were the tragic and inevitable results.
4. Though not without a strike involving about one third of the miners and the loss of over a million working days (Eric Wigham, *Strikes and the Government 1893–1974* (London: Macmillan, 1976) p. 176).
5. *The Economist*, 13 February 1971. This was awarded on the recommendation of a Court of Inquiry headed by Lord Wilberforce.
6. BBC producer, who wished to remain anonymous, in an interview with the author, 1974.
7. For a copy of Arthur Scargill's Operations Map and a description of his organization of the picketing at Saltley, see Clutterbuck, *Britain in Agony*, pp. 62–76.

8. Alan Law, 'The Miners are Coming', *The Miner*, April 1972. He gives a vivid and emotional picture of the last day at Saltley.
9. Interview in the *New Left Review*, September 1975.
10. *Observer Magazine*, 17 June 1979.

CHAPTER 3: GRUNWICK

1. Grunwick figures compiled from daily reports in *The Times* from 14 June to 12 July and from the *Sunday Times* and *Observer* of 26 June 1977. For Saltley figures see previous chapter. There were 14 civilian injuries reported at Saltley. There is no reliable record of civilian injuries at Grunwick. Figures for civilian injuries in demonstrations are in any case misleading as minor injuries to demonstrators are seldom reported whereas policemen on duty are obliged to report all injuries, however slight.
2. *Sunday Times*, 26 June 1977.
3. For a full account of the Grunwick dispute see Joe Rogaly, *Grunwick* (Harmondsworth: Penguin, 1977) and Lord Justice Scarman, *Report of Inquiry into the Dispute between the Grunwick Processing Laboratories and Members of APEX*, Cmnd 6922 (London: HMSO, 1977). Also Clutterbuck, *Britain in Agony*, ch. 16.
4. This attention was not wholly favourable. Right-wing papers castigated them, as ministers, for publicly taking sides in an industrial dispute. From the far left, *Socialist Worker* on 23 May derided their visit: 'Enough to make you want to throw up . . . stayed just long enough to have their picture taken.'
5. *Socialist Worker*, 11 June 1977.
6. *The Times*, 14 June 1977.
7. *Observer*, 26 June 1977.
8. A Press Association photograph showing this was printed in the first edition of Clutterbuck's *Britain in Agony* (London: Faber and Faber, 1978, facing p. 192). This shows what appears to be a predominantly student crowd bending the police cordon in front of a car. The placards with the 'scab' photographs are held up on poles by demonstrators at the back.
9. *The Times*, 21 June 1977.
10. *The Times*, 22 June 1977.
11. *The Times*, 23 June 1977.
12. *The Times*, 28 June 1977.
13. Figures given by the Home Secretary in Parliament and quoted by *The Times*, 29 June 1977.
14. *Listener*, 30 June 1977.
15. Home Secretary's figures in *The Times*, 29 June 1977,
16. *The Times*, 24 June 1977.
17. *Sunday Times*, 26 June 1977.
18. *Socialist Worker*, 2 July 1977.
19. *The Times*, Parliamentary Report, 15 July 1977.
20. *Daily Telegraph*, 23 July 1977.
21. *The Times*, 9 August 1977.
22. *Daily Telegraph*, 12 January 1978.

23. *Daily Telegraph*, 15 July 1978.
24. In a later interview on Granada Television's *Union Power* on 22 June 1980, Jack Dromey admitted that the bulk of those at Grunwick were not strikers but demonstrators, though he claimed that such a demonstration against the (then Labour) Government's policies was quite justified.

CHAPTER 4: THE WINTER OF DISCONTENT:
STRIKES AND THE PUBLIC

1. *Labour Research* is the title both of the organization and of its magazine. It is not, despite its title, directly connected with the Labour Party, though it has a number of Tribune Group members, including MPs, on its editorial board. It is run, in fact, by a mixture of Labour left wingers and members of the Communist Party.
2. J. M. Wober, *Television Coverage of Industrial Conflict: Viewers Perceptions of any Bias in Main News Coverage of Industrial Disputes in the Early Months of 1979* (London: IBA, May 1979) (hereafter IBA, *Viewers Perceptions*).
3. *Coverage of the Industrial Situation in January and February 1979* (London: BBC, February 1980) (hereafter BBC, *Coverage*). BBC, February 1980. The BBC General Advisory Council comprises 54 members including employers, trade unionists, MPs, journalists, writers, economists, police officers and others under the Chairmanship of Sir Frank Figgures, himself a former Director-General of NEDO and Chairman of the Pay Board. The author was a member of the GAC and of its Business Committee which requested the study and commented on the draft during its preparation. He also took part in the debate, but minutes of the Councils debates are non-attributable and not published.
4. BBC, *The Editors*, 30 June 1980. Participants included one of the authors of *More Bad News* (Paul Walton), a Communist Party trade union official (Ken Gill) and a number of industrial editors and other journalists from newspapers and the BBC.
5. Headlines taken from those recorded in *Labour Research*, April 1979 and *Cause for Concern*.
6. BBC, *Coverage*, p. 12.
7. For full details, including the different attitudes to different strikes (transport, hospital workers, refuse collectors, etc.) and perceptions of people with different political affiliations see IBA, *Viewers Perceptions*.
8. BBC, *Coverage*, p. 14.
9. IBA, *Viewers Perceptions*, p. 14.
10. See BBC, *Coverage* and IBA, *Viewers Perceptions*.
11. IBA Audience Research Department, *Attitudes to the Television Coverage of Industrial and Economic Affairs* (London: IBA, March 1977) (hereafter IBA, *Attitudes*, 1977). This survey also supported the later finding in *Viewers Perceptions* that the majority of viewers felt that news and current affairs programmes were 'rarely or never' biased towards either employers or trade unions.
12. This problem is fully examined in BBC, *Coverage*.

13. The violence at Saltley was mild compared with that in political demonstrations, including Grunwick, not because of the media, but because the miners picketing at Saltley did not have the intensity of hatred against the police which the demonstrators had. This hatred between the mainly university educated demonstrators and the police is examined in the next section of the book.

CHAPTER 5: POLITICAL DEMONSTRATIONS

1. Sir Robert Mark, 'The Metropolitan Police and Political Demonstrations', *Police Journal*, July—September 1975.
2. James D. Halloran, Philip Elliott and Graham Murdock, *Demonstrations and Communications: A Case Study* (Harmondsworth: Penguin, 1970).
3. There was an outstanding 30-minute *World in Action* report.
4. He later wrote that he regretted this decision and that he should have gone to Grosvenor Square to have the confrontation. Tariq Ali, *The Coming Revolution in Britain* (London: Jonathan Cape, 1972) pp. 158—9.
5. The Metropolitan Police concentrated a force of 9000 in the area of the march, but only 3000 were deployed, the remainder remaining in mobile reserve in their coaches.
6. Halloran *et al.*, *Demonstrations*, pp. 47—9. He records that 15 per cent of those taking part were non-British and that 75 per cent were students.
7. Lord Justice Scarman, *The Red Lion Square Disorders of 15 June, 1974*, Cmnd 5919 (London: HMSO, February 1975) p. 7.
8. See Clutterbuck, *Britain in Agony*, pp. 224—6 and 341.
9. *The Times*, 9 September 1976.
10. In an interview in 1977.
11. The original Rastafarian religion envisaged a black king who would lead the black people to their rightful place in the world. When Ras Tafari (Haile Selassie) acceded to the throne of Ethiopia, he was identified as that king. The religion did not encourage violence, though it did perhaps arouse a rather bitter yearning for greatness. These yearnings can be accurately described as racist (black superiority) but were not vicious in their religious form. They were, however, perverted by some of the leaders in the black communities in Jamaica and Britain to arouse young blacks to develop an aggressive pride and to demonstrate their superiority, especially their physical superiority, over the whites. As with football hooligans, they began to express this pride, first with colours and forms of hair style and dress, and then by violence.
12. Examples are given in Clutterbuck, *Britain in Agony*, p. 228.
13. Ibid., pp. 230—2. See, for example, the ten-page justification of violence in SWP's monthly journal *International Socialism*, September 1977.
14. Clutterbuck, *Britain in Agony*, p. 233.
15. National Council for Civil Liberties, *Southall 23 April 1979: The Report of the Unofficial Committee of Enquiry* (London: NCCL, 1980).

CHAPTER 6: REPORTING THE POLICE

1. William Belson, *The Public and the Police* (London: Harper Row, 1975).

2. See, for example, *Sunday Times*, 16 March 1980.
3. See, for example, interview with Arthur Scargill in *New Left Review*, September 1975, in which he describes his attitude to the police in the Saltley Coke Depot incident in 1972. See also the comment of the Communist Party shop steward on page 13.
4. For an excellent case study of policing in a high immigrant area see John Brown, *Shades of Grey* (Cranfield College of Technology, 1978).
5. *The Times*, 30 June 1980.
6. See, for example, NCCL, *Southall 23 April 1979*, pp. 38−42 and 149−50.
7. The police could obviously not give evidence before this unofficial inquiry because, regardless of any ethical considerations, there were still cases which were *sub judice* and the official public inquiry (in the form of an inquest) was still not completed.
8. Katharine Whitehorn, 'The New Law of Gravity' in the *Observer*, 13 July 1980.
9. *Police Review*, 18 July 1980. Lord Devlin's views were also summarized in *The Times*, 22 July 1980.
10. BBC TV, *Dimbleby Lecture*, 3 November 1973.
11. *The Times*, 11 July 1980.

CHAPTER 7: TELEVISION DOCUMENTARIES AND DRAMA

1. *The Listener*, 28 June 1979.
2. *Spectator*, 22 April 1978.
3. Percy Tannenbaum, *Research Related to Television Production* (London: BBC, 1980).
4. See Lord Devlin's comments on pages 71−2.
5. *The Prisoner's Tale* threw away a good chance of a realistic examination of the problem of an implacably recalcitrant prisoner. The play presented the problem very well but the solution it portrayed was totally incredible to anyone who knows the inside of a prison, notwithstanding the colourful tales which ex-prisoners will understandably like to tell (and sell) when they come out. The author of this book has been a fairly frequent visitor to prisons and Borstals, amongst some very violent inmates. In Wakefield, for example, over 250 of the 700 inmates have personally killed someone, yet the atmosphere in the evenings, with all except those in solitary confinement mingling freely with each other and the prison officers during the long association period, is amazingly relaxed. They have a very easy relationship and are not ashamed of this being seen by others. Quite apart from the un-likelihood of the widespread conspiracy that would be needed for the scenes depicted in Jack Lynn's cell, the atmosphere in the prison as a whole in *The Prisoner's Tale* bears no resemblance to reality at all.
6. BBC TV, *The Truth Game*, 22 June 1979, reproduced in the *Listener*, 28 June 1979.
7. Interestingly, Alan Plater wrote the script for a film version of *All Creatures Great and Small*.
8. This paper was being prepared for publication at the time this book went to press.

9. *Listener*, 28 June 1979.

CHAPTER 8: DISCLOSE OR DISCREDIT?

1. *Observer*, 13 July 1980.
2. Yorkshire Television, *A Force to Reckon With*, 2 July 1980.

CHAPTER 9: THE IRA AND THE MEDIA

1. Figures from Royal Ulster Constabulary monthly statistics, February 1980.
2. See page 93–4.
3. *Guardian* reporter Simon Winchester, in *In Holy Terror* (London: Faber and Faber, 1974) pp. 182–4, describes a hasty retreat from an interview with provisional IRA members when a telephone call from IRA Headquarters warned them that he might be spying for the British.
4. But see the quotations from Richard Francis and Simon Winchester on pages 105–6.
5. See Chapter 11.
6. Interview with Brigadier P. Hudson in Belfast, 1970.
7. *War Office Record of the Rebellion in Ireland*, Vol. II (London: HMSO, 1922) p. 46, quoted in Maurice Tugwell, 'Revolutionary Propaganda and Possible Countermeasures' (unpublished Defence Fellowship Thesis 1979, p. 233).
8. *Report of the Committee on the Future of Broadcasting*, Cmnd 6753 (Annan) (London: HMSO, 1977) p. 270.
9. Maria McGuire, *To Take Arms* (London: Macmillan, 1973). She describes how in 1971, when she joined, they arranged for Colin Smith, of the *Observer* to interview her 'as an example of the new type of middle class member the movement was attracting' (p. 19).
10. I. D. Evans, 'Public Relations Practice within the Army' (unpublished paper, National Defence College, Latimer, 1976).
11. Tugwell, 'Revolutionary Propaganda, pp. 236–7.
12. Interview with Alan Hooper recorded in his book *The Military and The Media* (MA thesis, Exeter University, to be published shortly).
13. *Report of the Tribunal appointed to inquire into the events on Sunday 30.1.72* (Widgery) HMSO (HL101, HC220) p. 14.
14. Widgery, ibid.
15. Deaths in 1972 were 467, compared with 175 the year before and 250 the year after. The next highest figure was 296 in 1976. Figures from Richard Clutterbuck, 'Northern Ireland: Is there a Way?', *Washington Review*, April 1978.

CHAPTER 10: THE POLICE AND THE ARMY IN NORTHERN IRELAND

1. Tugwell's thus far unpublished thesis on this subject is probably the best

analysis so far in the English language of the problems of dealing with revolutionary propaganda. The problems of the military and the media in this and also in a wider context, are fully discussed by Alan Hooper, *The Military and the Media*.

2. Named after the officer who signed the covering document.
3. See, for example, *Daily Telegraph*, 11 and 12 May 1979.
4. This account of the Dunloy incident is largely based on research by Alan Hooper, supplemented by interviews with some of those involved. For a fuller account see Alan Hooper, *The Military and the Media*.
5. *Daily Telegraph*, 12 July 1978.
6. See the *Sunday Times* of 16 July and 13 August 1978.
7. Statement released by HQ Northern Ireland and quoted in *Daily Telegraph*, 5 July 1979.
8. Richard Francis, *Broadcasting to a Community in Conflict* (London: BBC, 1977) p. 10.
9. Ibid.
10. Robin Walsh, 'Terrorism and Media' in RUSI, *Ten Years of Terrorism* (London: RUSI, 1979) p. 90.
11. Anne McHardy in the *Guardian*, 23 February 1980.
12. *The Times*, 27 February 1976.
13. Simon Winchester, *In Holy Terror*, p. 142.
14. Richard Francis, *Broadcasting to a Community in Conflict*, pp. 14–15.
15. *The Times*, 16 February 1976.

CHAPTER 11: ACCESS TO THE MEDIA FOR TERRORISTS

1. Richard Francis, *Broadcasting to a Community in Conflict*, report of a lecture at the Royal Institute of International Affairs, London, on 22 February, 1977, published by the BBC, 1977 (hereafter referred to as Francis, *Conflict*) p. 6.
2. Richard Francis, 'Television Reporting Beyond the Pale', *Listener*, 27 March 1980 (hereafter Francis, 'Beyond the Pale').
3. Ibid., pp. 13–14. Francis mentions that in the same period there were the same number (18) of interviews with leaders of the Peace Movement.
4. For a report on this programme, see *Daily Telegraph*, 17 December 1977. It also included pictures of an IRA Active Service Unit training in Belfast.
5. Richard Francis, 'Terrorists on Television', BBC press release of a speech to the Broadcasting Press on 12 July 1979 (hereafter Francis, 'Terrorists').
6. BBC, *Tonight*, 5 July 1979.
7. Ibid.
8. Ian Trethowan, Director-General of the BBC, in a letter to the *Daily Telegraph*, 14 July 1979.
9. Francis, 'Terrorists'.
10. *Daily Telegraph*, 12 July 1979.
11. *Daily Telegraph*, 13 July 1979.
12. A summary of the proceedings was later published by the BBC.
13. Ian Trethowan, in a letter to the *Daily Telegraph*, 14 July 1979.
14. *Listener*, 20 June 1974.

15. See, for example Francis, 'Beyond the Pale'.
16. BBC, *The Editors*, 15 July 1979.
17. Francis, 'Beyond the Pale'.
18. BBC, *The Editors*, 15 July 1979.
19. *Observer*, 11 November 1979.
20. *Guardian*, 16 November 1979.
21. This was audible in the background of the film 'rushes'.
22. *Observer*, 11 November 1979.
23. This account was issued by the Provisional Sinn Fein Office in Dublin in *Irish Republican Information Services* on 10 November, but a similar version was in fact given direct to the Press Association and others by IRA sources in Belfast on 8 November and appeared in British newspapers on 9 November.
24. *Guardian*, 9 November 1979.
25. *Daily Telegraph*, 9 November 1979.
26. *Guardian*, 10 November 1979.
27. *Ariel* (BBC staff magazine) 21 November 1979.
28. *Guardian*, 21 November 1979.
29. Francis, 'Beyond the Pale'.
30. *Economist*, 17 November 1979.
31. This is a paraphrase of extracts from the Act. For the full wording, and for a review of the effectiveness of the Act and its effect on liberties of the subject, see Lord Shackleton, *Review of the Operation of the Prevention of Terrorism (Temporary Provisions) Acts 1974 and 1976*, Cmnd 7324 (London: HMSO, 1978).
32. ITV, *State of the Nation*, 22 July 1979.

CHAPTER 12: KIDNAPPING

1. Caroline Moorehead, *Fortune's Hostages* (London: Hamish Hamilton, 1979) pp. ix–xi.
2. One of the five, Gabriele Kröcher-Tiedemann, within a year killed at least two more people (at the kidnapping of the OPEC oil ministers in Vienna) before she was eventually rearrested in Switzerland in January 1978 – a strong argument against the release of convicted terrorists as a bargain for the life of a hostage.
3. Quoted by Caroline Moorehead, *Fortune's Hostages*, p. 181.
4. For fuller accounts of the handling of the Schleyer case see Richard Clutterbuck, *Kidnap and Ransom* (London: Faber and Faber, 1978) and Caroline Moorehead *Fortune's Hostages, passim*.
5. The word kidnap can include seizure of children in divorce disputes, captives in gang warfare or other short-term abductions. The examples considered in this chapter are only those sufficiently 'major' to attract wide media interest, and in which that interest has influenced the course of events.
6. Sir Robert Mark, 'Kidnapping, Terrorism and the News Media in Britain' in Royal United Services Institute, *Ten Years of Terrorism* (London: RUSI, 1979) p. 76.
7. The story of these operations is told more fully in Richard Clutterbuck's *Riot and Revolution in Singapore and Malaya* (London: Faber and Faber, 1973)

pp. 252–7. The author was a member of the Director of Operations Staff throughout the 'Political Commissar' operation and at the start of the Hor Lung Operation. Nine years later (1967) he returned to Malaya and met Hor Lung and some of his comrades while doing research for that book. Hor Lung was still living in Johore, to all appearances quite openly, running a prosperous business capitalized by the substantial reward he received. His erstwhile comrades seemed to bear him no ill will, as they now recognized that by 1958 their war had been lost and that, but for his action, most of the 160 he led out of the jungle would almost certainly otherwise have died there.

8. *Daily Telegraph*, 30 August 1979.
9. The author took part in this programme (*Nationwide*, 10 September 1979) on the end of a landline from the Plymouth studio. When asked to do so he said that he would only discuss kidnapping generally, and urged the programme staff not to discuss the Schild case specifically since such discussion could not possibly help him or his family but could most certainly increase their danger and give their kidnappers information they were unlikely otherwise to acquire. He then sat, furious and frustrated, his microphone not yet live, watching on the monitor what was going out on the air, unable to intervene. Had he been in the London studio he would have cut in himself as soon as the line of discussion emerged, questioning the propriety of continuing it. Had it been recorded even only a few minutes earlier (as is often done on, for example, BBC Radio's *World at One*) the wisdom of transmitting it could at least have been reconsidered.
10. *Daily Telegraph*, 30 August 1979.
11. *Sunday Times*, 23 March 1980.
12. *Sunday Times*, 6 January 1980.

CHAPTER 13: SIEGE AND RESCUE

1. Frank Bolz, in an interview with the author, March 1976.
2. At the BBC conference attended by the author in Abingdon in November 1979 (see page 113), one of the 'hypothetical' situations explored was an embassy siege in London. British and American press and television reporters said that they would do their utmost to get round any attempt by the police to 'sterilize' the area, that they would immediately seek out windows or roofs from which to aim their cameras, and would pay large sums, on the spot, to contract for the use of these vantage points. They stressed that they regarded any restraint as up to them and that, while they were prepared to listen to requests for such restraint, any attempt to impose it against their will would be resisted.
3. BBC, *The Editors*, 16 June 1980.
4. *Observer* staff, *Siege* (London: Macmillan, 1980) p. 31.
5. *The Editors*, 16 June 1980.
6. *Siege*, p. 93.
7. *Observer*, 11 May 1980.
8. Another example of the police appreciating the calming effect of appeasing the terrorists' desire for publicity occurred in the hijacking of a train by South Moluccan terrorists in the Netherlands in December 1975. After the siege

had lasted for twelve days one of the hostages, Hans Prinz, realized that the terrorists were becoming dangerously frustrated because they had no idea what was going on outside. Prinz persuaded the police to pass a transistor radio into the train. The terrorists discovered, to their surprise, the extent to which they had achieved their aim of publicity of their cause, and they surrendered within a few hours.

CHAPTER 14: LIVING WITH THE MEDIA

1. Denis MacShane, *Using the Media* (London: Pluto Press, 1979).
2. See page 14.
3. MacShane, *Using the Media*, p. 1.
4. BBC, *Tonight*, 28 April 1978.
5. *New Yorker*, 12 June 1978.
6. See pages 75—6.
7. *Daily Telegraph*, 19 June 1979. For a full account of the making of *Sailor*, *Warship* and *Spearhead*, see Alan Hooper, *The Military and the Media* (MA thesis, Exeter University, to be published shortly).
8. MacShane, *Using the Media*, p. 147.

Bibliography

ALEXANDER, YONAH (ed.) *Terrorism, An International Journal*, vol. 2, nos 1, 2 (New York: Crane Russak, 1979). This volume discusses terrorism and the media. It is the edited proceedings of two conferences in America on this subject, one on 'Terrorism: Police and Press Problems' (1976) and the other on 'Terrorism and the Media' (1977). Participants were academics, newsmen and security men.

ANNAN, LORD, *Report of the Committee on the Future of Broadcasting*, Cmnd 6753 (London: HMSO, 1977). The Report of the Annan committee covering all aspects of broadcasting from the fourth channel to children's viewing.

BBC, *The Task of Broadcasting News* (London: BBC, 1976). Originally a paper produced for the BBC General Advisory Council, it examines the controversies over news production, the principles and practices followed by BBC journalists and includes contributions from regional stations.

BBC, *Coverage of the Industrial Situation in January and February 1979* (London: BBC, 1980). A report for the GAC of the BBC's coverage of the 'winter of discontent', looked at in the light of the criticisms of media bias against trade unions and strikers.

BBC, *The Editors* (Television programmes, 15 July 1979, 16 and 30 June 1980). Series of discussions by a panel of editors and journalists, including the media treatment of the INLA interview (15 July 1979), the Iranian Embassy Siege (16 June 1980) and of industrial disputes (30 June 1980).

BBC, *The Truth Game* (Television programme, 22 June 1979). Discussion of *Law and Order* drama series.

BBC Handbook (London: BBC, annually). Annual review of what has gone on in the BBC and the broadcasting world.

BEHARRELL, PETER and PHILO, GREG (eds), *Trade Unions and the Media* (London: Macmillan, 1977). A collection of essays on the way the trade unions are presented by the media. The authors

176

(many of the Glasgow Media Group) argue that the trade unions are unfavourably portrayed, being consistently shown as the cause of our economic problems. They suggest that this picture is given as it is in the interest of the small group of owners and managers of the media, and that alternative explanations for our economic troubles are therefore seldom aired.

BELOFF, NORA, *Freedom under Foot* (London: Temple Smith, 1976). The story of the passage of Michael Foot's Closed Shop Bill through Parliament in 1976 and its implications for editorial freedom.

BELSON, WILLIAM, *Television Violence and Adolescent Boys* (Farnborough: Saxon House, 1978). The results of an investigation into the effects on male adolescents of long-term exposure to television violence, concluding that high exposure increases the degree to which boys engage in serious violence.

BIRT, JOHN and JAY, PETER, *The Times*, 28 February 1975 (Birt alone), 30 September 1975, 1 October 1975. The three articles which introduced the now famous phrase 'a bias against understanding' which is what they argue television produces in its present form, where news is separate from current affairs and more comprehensive explanations of reports.

BRIGGS, ASA, *The History of Broadcasting in the United Kingdom*, 4 vols (London: Oxford University Press, 1979). An extremely detailed, authoritative history of broadcasting from its beginnings, relating its history to the history of British society.

CHIBNALL, STEVE, *Law and Order News* (London: Tavistock Publications, 1977). A study of how crime, social deviancy and the forces of order are dealt with in the press; of how the journalists in this field come by their information and shape it for publication, and how the police (and the army in Northern Ireland) handle the press.

CLARK, M. J. (ed.), *Politics and the Media* (Oxford: Pergamon, 1979). A collection of essays on various topics from film to television. Contains an essay by Robert Hargreaves, then Home Affairs Correspondent, ITN, arguing for complete impartiality in news with no bias in favour of the establishment or existing social mores.

CLUTTERBUCK, RICHARD, *Britain in Agony* (Harmondsworth: Penguin, 1980). Describes the background and events in some of the case-studies.

CURRAN, CHARLES, *BBC Journalism: The Relevance of Structures*

(London: BBC, 1977). A lecture supporting the separation of news from current affairs, a separation which is not now strictly in operation as *Newsnight* combines the two.

CURRAN, CHARLES, *A Seamless Robe* (London: Collins, 1979). The BBC through the eyes of one of their past Director-Generals.

CURRAN, CHARLES, YOUNG, BRIAN and ANNAN, LORD, *Television, Today and Tomorrow*, The Granada Guildhall Lectures 1977 (St Albans: Granada, 1977). Lectures on Reports of Broadcasting Committees, particularly the Annan proposals.

CURRAN, JAMES (ed.), *The British Press: A Manifesto* (London: Macmillan, 1978). Essays by academics and newsmen on different aspects of the press and newspaper journalism – ownership, censorship, law, technology, etc.

CURRAN, JAMES, GUREVITCH, MICHAEL and WOOLLACOT, JANET (eds.), *Mass Communication and Society* (London: Edward Arnold, 1977). A collection of essays, mainly by academics, on the media and their relationship with society and politics, in the past and present.

DAY, ROBIN, *Day by Day* (London: William Kimber, 1975). An autobiographical account, some written in self-interview form, of Day's career, experiences and views on television. He argues that television should be used to support a reasonable society by having more reasoned debate and fewer sensational presentations of violence and irrational acts.

DRESNER, STEWART, *Open Government: Lessons from America* (London: Outer Circle Policy Unit, 1980). An examination of the American Freedom of Information Act and open government in general, which he concludes has ensured that the United States executive has been subject to a more effective public scrutiny and has also inhibited corruption.

EYSENCK, H. J. and NIAS, D. K., *Sex, Violence and the Media* (London: Temple Smith, 1978). A study of the effect on boys of watching sex and violence on television, concluding that aggressive acts on television can cause young viewers to imitate them. They argue that censorship can therefore be justified, though hope it can be brought about by self-restraint.

FISKE, JOHN and HARTLEY, JOHN, *Reading Television* (London: Methuen, 1978). A study of the method by which television communicates using linguistic and semiotic terms and methodology.

FRANCIS, RICHARD *Broadcasting to a Community in Conflict*

(London: BBC, 1977). A lecture outlining the problems of broadcasting in Northern Ireland.

FRANCIS, RICHARD, 'Television Reporting Beyond the Pale', *Listener*, 27 March 1980. A justification of interviewing terrorists on television.

THE GLASGOW UNIVERSITY MEDIA GROUP, *Bad News* (London: Routledge and Kegan Paul, 1976) *and*

THE GLASGOW UNIVERSITY MEDIA GROUP, *More Bad News* (London: Routledge and Kegan Paul, 1980). The results of a survey of six months of television news in 1975. The authors found that television interpreted events mainly from one narrow viewpoint. Economic reporting, for example, tended to take the Treasury line, reflecting the view of the government of the day. Wage restraint was put forward as virtually the only solution to inflation. News language favoured employers who were reported as making 'pleas' or 'offers' whereas unions were frequently reported as making 'demands' or 'threats'.

GRANADA, *State of the Nation* (Television programme, 22 July 1979). Programme of discussion between many newsmen and security people on the reporting of terrorism and violence.

HALLORAN, JAMES, ELLIOT, PHILIP and MURDOCK, GRAHAM, *Demonstrations and Communication – A Case Study* (Harmondsworth: Penguin, 1970). An examination of media coverage of the anti-Vietnam War demonstration in Grosvenor Square in 1968. The authors found that the media's predictions of the form of the demonstration influenced the way they subsequently portrayed it. The media had a tendency to fill any gaps in their knowledge of events with what they had thought was going to happen. They thus concentrated on the violence and aggression and produced a somewhat distorted image of the whole.

HMSO, *White Paper on Broadcasting*, Cmnd 7294 (London: HMSO, 1978). Government proposals for the future of broadcasting after the Annan Report.

HOOPER, ALAN, *The Military and the Media* (MA thesis, Exeter University). An analysis of the successes and failures of the armed forces in dealing with the media. Includes a concise and lucid account of how news is gathered for newspapers and broadcasting, and how radio and TV news, current affairs, documentaries and drama programmes are made.

IBA (J. M. Wober), *Attitudes to Television Coverage of Industrial and Economic Affairs* (London: IBA, March 1977). An audience research survey which found that the majority of viewers did not consider news and current affairs coverage of industrial disputes to be biased.

IBA (J. M. Wober), *Television Coverage of Industrial Conflict: Viewers' Perceptions of any Bias in Main News Coverage of Industrial Disputes in the Early Months of 1979* (London: IBA, May 1979). Similar findings to the above for the coverage of the disputes of early 1979.

INSTITUTE FOR THE STUDY OF CONFLICT, *Television and Conflict* (London: ISC, November 1978). A report of a conference whose participants included Robert Mark, Anthony Howard, Brian Crozier, Keith Kyle and Lord Chalfont. Covers the problems of reporting terrorism, undeclared wars, and situations like Grunwick. It also examines the difficulties of dealing with extremist propaganda.

JAEHNIG, WALTER B., 'Journalists and Terrorism: Captives of the Libertarian Tradition', *Indiana Law Journal*, vol. 53, no. 4 (1977–8). An interesting paper on the relations of these two, concentrating on American examples. Examines journalistic ethics and the problems that libertarianism and its required objectivity produce when reporting situations where lives are at stake.

JENKINS, SIMON, *Newspapers: The Power and the Money* (London: Faber and Faber, 1979). A history of newspapers, their control and the changing character of proprietors. New newspaper technology and the press's reaction to it are also discussed.

KATZ, ELIHU, *Social Research on Broadcasting: Proposals for Further Development* (London: BBC, 1977). Written for the BBC, this is a comprehensive and scholarly report of the state of media research in 1977 and makes suggestions for its future path.

KNIGHTLEY, PHILLIP, *The First Casualty* (London: Andre Deutsch, 1975). A thorough history of the war correspondent, a perilous post which many of the top journalists have held at one time.

LEICESTER CENTRE FOR MASS COMMUNICATION AND RESEARCH, *Current British Research on Mass Media and Mass Communication* (December 1979, annually). Register of ongoing and recently completed research.

LEVIN, BERNARD, *The Levin Interviews* (Television programme, 3 May 1980). An interview with Robin Day on BBC Television.

MCQUAIL, DENIS, *Towards a Sociology of Mass Communications*

(London: Collier, Macmillan, 1969). Links together many of the studies of mass communications and discusses major themes; whether mass communications produce a mass society, how audiences respond to different media and how the media could be used and developed.

MACSHANE, DENIS, *Using the Media: Workers' Handbook* (London: Pluto Press, 1979). A guide for workers by a journalist on how to go about getting their case best put over in the media. It is therefore also useful as an insight into how the media operate.

MARGACH, JAMES, *The Abuse of Power* (London: W. H. Allen, 1978). An account from the personal knowledge of a former *Sunday Times* Political Correspondent of the relationship between Prime Ministers (from Lloyd-George to Callaghan) with the press and television, demonstrating the importance of the media for those in power.

MARK, ROBERT, *In the Office of Constable* (London: Collins, 1978). Autobiography of ex-Commissioner of the Metropolitan Police, whose term spanned the Spaghetti House and Balcombe Street sieges. It includes one chapter on the police and the media, where he maintains that mutual co-operation would benefit both.

MUNRO, COLIN R., *Television, Censorship and the Law* (Farnborough: Saxon House, 1979). A survey of all the infringements on the complete freedom of the media, particularly the legal ones.

NATIONAL COUNCIL FOR CIVIL LIBERTIES, *Southall 23rd April 1979: The Report of the Unofficial Committee of Enquiry* (London: NCCL, 1980). Investigates the events in Southall when a demonstration against a NF meeting developed into a riot. (The NCCL did not get police co-operation for their enquiry.) It has a chapter on the media and the way they reported Southall.

OBSERVER, THE, *Siege* (London: Macmillan, 1980). A good 'instant paperback' on the Iranian Embassy siege in London. It covers the media aspects well.

PINCHER, CHAPMAN, *Inside Story* (London: Sidgwick and Jackson, 1978). A personal account by one of the longest serving defence correspondents and investigative journalists. An interesting insight into the relationship between journalists and their sources in the political world.

ROGALY, JOE, *Grunwick* (Harmondsworth: Penguin, 1977).

Another good 'instant paperback' on the Grunwick dispute by an experienced journalist.

ROYAL UNITED SERVICES INSTITUTE FOR DEFENCE STUDIES, *Ten Years of Terrorism* (London: RUSI, 1979). Contributions given at a series of meetings in 1977 including one on the media and terrorism by Martin Bell and Robin Walsh (BBC Northern Ireland) and on the same subject but referring to Britain by Sir Robert Mark.

SCHLESINGER, PHILIP, *Putting 'Reality' Together: BBC News* (London: Constable, 1978). A study of the BBC's production of news and current affairs (an interpretation which was not very favourably received by the BBC). Examines the nature of BBC impartiality and those whose job it is to maintain it.

SIMS, MONICA, *The Portrayal of Violence in Television Programmes* (London: BBC, 1979). A report written for the BBC which discusses the arguments and contributions to the debate as to whether the portrayal of violence on television causes violent behaviour.

SMITH, ANTHONY, *The Politics of Information* (London: Macmillan, 1972). A collection of his articles which concern the political implications of media policy. He thinks that the mass media, instead of producing an informed mass democracy have created a gap between the informed elite and the rest who mainly seek entertainment rather than information. There is an interesting chapter on the history of broadcasting in Northern Ireland.

Sunday Times, 23 March 1980. A major article on the early stage of the Schild kidnap which illustrates the effects that media reports had on the course of the kidnap.

SWANN, MICHAEL, *Broadcasting Blues* (London: BBC, 1975). Pamphlet of a lecture on the problems of the news being all gloom and how good news might be 'news' too.

SWANN, MICHAEL, *Are the Lamps Going Out?* (London: BBC, 1977). A lecture on the threats to the freedom of speech and the media's role in its maintenance.

TANNENBAUM, PERCY, *Research Related to Television Production* (London: BBC, 1980). A project sponsored by the BBC to study the effects on their audiences of three BBC programme series, including the *Law and Order* drama series.

TAYLOR, DESMOND, *Editorial Responsibilities* (London: BBC, 1975). A lecture on the methods journalists and editors employ to arrive at their reports on such issues as industrial affairs and Northern Ireland.

TRACEY, MICHAEL, *The Production of Political Television* (London: Routledge and Kegan Paul, 1978). A study of television through interviews and observation of producers at work. Also some archival studies of e.g. the BBC and the General Strike, *Yesterday's Men*. Tries to find if and where the political influences and pressures on broadcasting are.

TRAINI, ROBERT, 'Police and the Press', *Police Review*, 15 June 1979. A fairly long article by an experienced crime reporter on how the police and the journalists get on together, noting the difference in attitude to the press of the uniformed police and the CID, and the changing attitude in the police force to the press. Records some of the incidents where there was considerable police/press co-operation e.g. Cypriot girl's kidnap, and the non-reporting of bomb hoaxes.

TUC, *How to Handle the Media: A Guide for Trade Unionists* (London: TUC, 1979). A guide for trade unionists on how to handle the media and how to get their case put over favourably.

TUC, *A Cause for Concern* (London: TUC, 1979). Examines the media coverage of industrial disputes in January and February 1979 to find out how and why the strikers got unfavourable coverage.

TUGWELL, MAURICE, 'Revolutionary Propaganda and Possible Countermeasures' (unpublished Defence Fellowship Thesis, Ministry of Defence, London 1979). Six case studies, including Algeria, Ireland (1916 and the 1970s) and Oman, leading to an analysis of the pattern of revolutionary propaganda and of countermeasures.

TUNSTALL, JEREMY (ed.), *Media Sociology* (London, Constable, 1970). A collection of essays on various topics concerning the media.

WESKER, ARNOLD, *Journey into Journalism* (London: Writers and Readers Publishing Co-operative, 1977). A portrayal of newspaper life and production based on visits to the *Sunday Times*.

WHALE, JOHN, *The Politics of the Media* (London: Fontana/Collins, 1977). A journalist's account of the media from 1945, describing the pressures and influences on the media, the owners, the advertisers; the unions and the state and the law.

WILLIAMS, RAYMOND, *Television: Technology and Cultural Form*

(London: Fontana/Collins, 1974). A study of television technology and its consequences on the form television presentations and portrayals of society take.

WINCHESTER, SIMON, *In Holy Terror* (London: Faber and Faber, 1974). An account by the then *Guardian* Northern Ireland correspondent describing the early seventies in Northern Ireland and the pressures and problems of reporting there.

WINDLESHAM, LORD, *Broadcasting in a Free Society* (Oxford: Blackwell, 1980). An analysis by the Managing Director of ATV, written during the production of ATV's controversial programme *Death of a Princess*, in which he argues for freedom from government interference, while stressing the need for broadcasters to show responsibility.

WYNDHAM GOLDIE, GRACE, *Facing the Nation* (London: The Bodley Head, 1977). An account of the early days of the BBC up to 1976 from one of its senior members. She concentrates on television's relationship with politics and politicians.

YORKE, IVOR, *The Technique of Television News* (London: Focal Press, 1978). A detailed description of all the techniques required to bring the final product to the television screen, from positioning interviewees to editing films. Useful therefore for an understanding of the form television programmes take.

Index